3

Twayne's United States Authors Series

Larry McMurtry

TUSAS 291

LARRY MCMURTRY

CHARLES D. PEAVY

University of Houston

TWAYNE PUBLISHERS
A DIVISION OF G. K. HALL & CO., BOSTON

Library of Congress Cataloging in Publication Data

Peavy, Charles D.
  Larry McMurtry.

  (Twayne's United States authors series ; TUSAS 291)
  Bibliography: p. 127–41
  Includes index.
  1. McMurtry, Larry—Criticism and interpretation.
PS3563.A319Z8   813'.5'4   77-11191
ISBN 0-8057-7194-8

Contents

About the Author

Charles D. Peavy is a professor of English at the University of Houston, where he teaches undergraduate and graduate courses in American literature. Professor Peavy holds the B.A. degree and the M.A. degree from Louisiana State University and the Ph.D degree from Tulane University. He is the recipient of grants from the National Endowment for the Humanities, the American Philosophical Society, and the American Council of Learned Societies.

Dr. Peavy has published articles and monographs in the areas of American literature, Afro-American literature and popular culture. He is also a film critic and film maker.

Preface

The purpose of this study is to examine and evaluate the works of Larry McMurtry. In my investigation of McMurtry's writing, I seek to accomplish two things. First, I will analyze McMurtry's novels, showing his use of such traditional themes as the rites of passage, the fall from innocence, and initiation. Although I will concentrate primarily on McMurtry's six novels, I will also indicate how McMurtry's nonfiction elucidates themes and meaning that appear in his fiction. Second, I will place McMurtry's novels in the context of twentieth-century American literature and illustrate McMurtry's utilization and transformation of material found in the traditions of the Western, beat literature, and black humor, with his concomitant departure from the cowboy stereotypes in the creation of the modern Western novel and film, his demythification of the old West in his realistic portrayal of the region, and his innovative employment of black humor in a Western context.

Chapter 1, primarily biographical, is concerned with McMurtry's early life in a Texas ranching community and the effect the region had upon his writing, the early influence of the beat generation upon McMurtry while he was an undergraduate in college, and his early literary apprenticeship as a poet, essayist, and short-fiction writer.

Chapter 2 provides brief summaries and critical appraisals of McMurtry's novels. His first two, *Horseman, Pass By* and *Leaving Cheyenne*, are the most poignant fiction he has ever written; the omnipresent themes are loneliness and loss; the consistent tone is elegiac. The nostalgia for rural life evidenced in these first two novels is abruptly terminated in the searing attack on the small town in *The Last Picture Show*, a novel characterized by satire and black humor. *The Last Picture Show* signals the less symbolic and more sociological style employed in *Moving On* and *All My Friends Are Going To Be Strangers*, the first two books of McMurtry's urban trilogy. These two novels are about the dispossessed young descendants of the old society and their painful metamorphosis as they move from a rural tradition rooted in the soil to a highly mobile, urbanized environment. His last novel, *Terms of Endearment*, although linked superficially to the first two books in the urban trilogy, is stylistically atypical of his previous work. Despite an unfortuitous excursus into melodrama in book II, *Terms of Endearment* represents McMurtry's first attempt at a comedy of manners.

Chapter 3 examines the major themes found in McMurtry's fiction; initiation and loneliness, which characterize the maturation of the male protagonists in the first three novels; the dissolution of marriage, which, while present in all his novels, is particularly true of the displaced Texans caught up in the urban environments of *Moving On* and *All My Friends Are Going To Be Strangers;* and emphemerality, which is a repetitive motif in all the novels.

Chapter 4 examines McMurtry's characterizations, especially his female characters and the important role they play in his fiction. McMurtry's female characters typically dominate the action of his books, and often, particularly in the case of the older or more emotionally mature ones, they have important functions in the emotional development of the male characters.

Chapter 5 examines the importance of the movies and the motion picture industry to McMurtry's career and art. References to movies are frequent in *Moving On* and *All My Friends Are Going To Be Strangers* and are essential to the plot and theme of *The Last Picture Show*. A discussion of McMurtry's film criticism is also included. His published film criticism is listed separately in the bibliography.

Chapter 6 deals with McMurtry's contributions to contemporary literature, particularly in his innovative approaches to the traditional genre of the Western. McMurtry is preeminently a regionalist, perhaps the best the Southwest has yet produced, but his frank treatment of sex and his use of satire and black humor distinguish his art from that of his predecessors. Moreover, in his examination of rootless Texans in metropolitan environments in the later novels, McMurtry has perhaps created a new avatar of the genre, the urban Western.

Following the text is a bibliography of primary sources, including unpublished material, and critical studies of McMurtry. I have tried to present as definitive a bibliography as possible, including fugitive pieces and published and unpublished fragments because of the elucidation they afford in the study of McMurtry's major works.

CHARLES D. PEAVY

University of Houston

Acknowledgments

I would like to acknowledge my indebtedness to Larry McMurtry who, in conversations and interviews at his former home in Houston, Texas, and later at his bookshop in Washington, D.C., supplied me with biographical data and valuable information concerning his writing. He also provided me with copies of his fugitive pieces, which appeared in such periodicals as *The Colonial Times* and *The Daily Rag*. I am most grateful for his liberal permission to quote from his works. Acknowledgments are also due to Harper and Brothers for permission to quote passages from *Horseman, Pass By* and *Leaving Cheyenne*, to Dial Press for permission to quote passages from *The Last Picture Show*, to Simon and Schuster for permission to quote from *Moving On* and *All My Friends Are Going to Be Strangers*, and to the Encino Press for permission to quote from *In a Narrow Grave*. I wish to thank the editors of *Western American Literature* who allowed me to quote from my articles "Coming of Age in the Southwest: The Novels of Larry McMurtry" and "Larry McMurtry and Black Humor: A Note on *The Last Picture Show*."

The unpublished theses of Inez Hernandez Tovar and Jimmie Clifton Sniffen are informative in their comments on McMurtry's female characters, and the papers read by Billie Phillips and Paulene Degenfelder at a session I chaired at the Popular Culture Association convention were helpful in their comments on McMurtry's work.

I wish to thank Zelda Osborne of the University of Houston Libraries, who assisted me in purchasing an extensive McMurtry manuscript and correspondence collection now housed in the Special Collections at the University, and Marion Orgain, special collections librarian, who worked with me on these documents and who pointed out to me the source for an early, variant title of McMurtry's *Moving On*.

Acknowledgment is due to the American Philosophical Society for a grant which allowed me to fly to Washington, D.C. to interview McMurtry before the final preparation of the manuscript of this book, and to Professor Sylvan Karchmer and the University of Houston Publications Committee for funds.

Special thanks are due to Chris Morris for her patience and endurance while typing the final drafts of the manuscript and for her frequent and welcome encouragement to complete the project.

Finally, I want to acknowledge the valuable assistance of my wife, Professor Elysee Hamlett Peavy, who not only read the various drafts of the manuscript and offered constructive criticism during its preparation but also assisted me in the task of proofreading and indexing. Had it not been for her, the book would never have been completed, and for this—and so much more—I shall always be thankful.

Chronology

1936 Born June 3 in Wichita Falls, Texas.

1954 Graduated with honors, Archer City High School, Archer City, Texas.

1954 Enrolled at Rice University, Houston, Texas.

1955 Transferred to North Texas State University, Denton, Texas, February.

1957 Published fiction, nonfiction, and poetry in *Avesta*, North Texas State University literary magazine.

1957 Won first prize for essay and second prize for poem in the *Avesta* awards.

1958 Received B.A. degree, North Texas State University.

1958 Graduate work in English, Rice University, Houston.

1958 Fall, completed first draft of *Horseman, Pass By* (completed five more drafts between 1958 and 1961).

1959 Married Jo Scott, Missouri City, Texas, July.

1960 Received M.A. degree, Rice University.

1960– Wallace Stegner Fellowship, Stanford University.
1961

1961 *Horseman, Pass By* published by Harper & Row.

1961– Taught at Texas Christian University, Fort Worth.
1962

1963 *Hud*, movie adaptation of *Horseman, Pass By*, released by Paramount.

1963– Taught English and creative writing, Rice University.
1964

1963 *Leaving Cheyenne* published by Harper & Row.

1964– Received Guggenheim Award for creative writing.
1965

1965 Returned to teaching at Rice University.

1965 Became book scout and dealer for "The Bookman," Houston.

1966 Divorced, August.

1966 *The Last Picture Show* published by Dial Press.

1968 *In a Narrow Grave: Essays on Texas* published by Encino Press.

1969   Moved to Waterford, Virginia.
1970   Taught at George Mason College, spring semester.
1970   *Moving On* published by Simon & Schuster.
1970– Taught at American University.
1971
1971   *The Last Picture Show* (movie version) released.
1972   *All My Friends Are Going To Be Strangers* published by Simon & Schuster.
1973   *Lovin' Molly,* movie version of *Leaving Cheyenne,* released.
1975   *Terms of Endearment* published by Simon & Schuster.
1975   Became contributing editor, *American Film.*

CHAPTER 1

Early Life and Literary Apprenticeship

I Influence of West Texas Boyhood

L ARRY McMurtry, the son and grandson of Texas cattlemen, was born on June 3, 1936, in Wichita Falls, Texas, near Archer City, where he grew up. An honor student at Archer City High School, McMurtry displayed the diversified interests characteristic of the "well-rounded boy." On his graduation (1954) the local newspaper listed his accomplishments: four-year letterman in band; three-year letterman in basketball; one-year letterman in baseball; 4-H Club officer for four years; editorial writer on *Cat's Claw* staff; member of the cast of the junior class and senior class plays; fourth-place winner in the district mile race; second-place winner in editorial writing. Young McMurtry soon won many more honors, including three Texas Institute of Letters awards (the fiction prize for *Horseman, Pass By* in 1961, the periodical prose award for a 1965 *Holiday* magazine article, and the Jesse H. Jones award for *The Last Picture Show*), a Stanford University Fellowship in fiction (1960–61), and a Guggenheim award (1964).

Ironically, McMurtry's first three novels, all written before he was thirty, were not popular in Archer City, and book reviewers for his hometown paper were squeamish about reviewing them. When asked about the reception of his books, McMurtry told an interviewer, "They can hardly be said to have had a reception. Parents and a few friends have read them and registered some outrage but not very perceptive outrage. If anyone in the town thinks of me at all it is probably only with mild embarrassment . . . a nice boy grown inexplicably strange and a little nervous-making."[1] Many of the residents of McMurtry's hometown have been highly critical of him, and some have been overtly hostile. Although some of these attitudes are a reaction to McMurtry's frank depiction of sex in his fiction, more often than not they are in

13

response to his criticism, and even satire, of the region in *The Last Picture Show* and in his collection of essays, *In a Narrow Grave*.

Such attitudes are overly reactive and defensive, however, indicating a failure to perceive the subtleties of McMurtry's satire. There is always a tension in McMurtry's criticism of his region, an ambivalence that he himself notes in the closing essay of *In a Narrow Grave*, "Take My Saddle from the Wall: A Valediction" (pp. 141–142. "The reader who has attended thus far," he writes, "will have noticed a certain inconsistency in my treatment of Texas past and present—a contradiction of attractions, one might call it. . . . What in this book appear to be inconsistencies of attitude are the manifestations of my ambivalence in regard to Texas—and a very deep ambivalence is not helpful in a discursive book, but it can be the very blood of a novel."

The tension catalyzed by these ambivalences gives McMurtry's fiction its depth and his essays their seriousness; he is neither a romancer nor a mythmaker in the tradition of J. Frank Dobie, nor is he the "debunker" or "demythicizer" that some critics have claimed. Thomas Landess writes that McMurtry's first two novels (*Horseman, Pass By* and *Leaving Cheyenne*) "have established him among Texas' most successful mythmakers."[2] McMurtry, however, does not see the two novels as mythmaking. He has stated that he is very interested in mythology, particularly American mythology, but he considers his works as "embodying myths, rather than making them."[3] He agrees that all of his Western characters to some extent embody mythological attitudes connected with the cowboy and the old West, but he denies that he is consciously setting out to reinforce these myths or to destroy them.

McMurtry's consciousness was quite naturally imbued with myths when he was a child in west Texas. He often heard the stories of the legendary cowboys and cattlemen, of Charles Goodnight and Teddy Blue and his own cowboy forebears, related to him at family reunions by older McMurtry males, all of whom had "lived to see the ideals of the faith degenerate, the rituals fall from use, the principal myth become corrupt. In my youth, when they were old men, I often heard them yearn aloud for the days when the rituals had all their power, when they themselves had enacted the pure, the original myth, and I know that they found it bitter to leave the land to which they were always faithful to the strange and godless heirs that they had bred" (*In a Narrow Grave*, p. 143). McMurtry realized that these men represented something that was vanishing, and as a young man he could remain objective about its loss. He writes of them in "Valediction" "not to pay homage" but in "a gesture of recognition, a wave such as riders sometimes give one another as they start down opposite sides of a hill," the "kind of recognition that kinsmen are so frequently only able to make in a time of parting" (p. 143).

Undeniably, McMurtry's first three novels contain a sense of loss—a loss of innocence, or of youth, or of the land, or of a way of life. They convey regret over this loss but not without some mixed feeling—again reflecting the ambivalence so characteristic of McMurtry's writing. "I suppose it is a kind of bitter-sweet feeling," he has said. "I've not been particularly romantic about that way of life; I've been as critical of it as anyone has—and yet, there is a certain amount of affection mixed in with the criticism. On the one hand I am both affectionate and slightly nostalgic, yet on the other hand, not nostalgic."[4] When asked if his ambivalence was like that of Faulkner's Quentin Compson in *Absalom, Absalom,* who, speaking of the South, cried, "I don't hate it, I don't hate it," or even Faulkner's own agonized attitude about his South, McMurtry responded, "No, it's not that intense. I don't think any people are as intense about their place as Southerners are. On the other hand, I think my attitude is more realistic. I think the Southerner needs to dramatize. This is evident in their fiction as well as in their lives. Everything has to be dramatized more intensely in the South, and it really is, essentially. Southern writers will get drama into their lives and into their work even if they have to go crazy to do it, which is not a compulsion I feel."[5]

II *Undergraduate Writing at North Texas State*

After graduation from high school and a semester at Rice University in Houston, McMurtry attended North Texas State University in Denton, Texas, where he received the B.A. degree in 1958. During his junior and senior years at North Texas, McMurtry said, he wrote fifty-two "very bad" short stories ("I counted them the day I burned them") but finally, "in an effort to write one less appalling than the original 52," he began to utilize his cowboy background.[6] In his senior year he wrote two stories, one about the destruction of a cattle herd and another about a cattleman's funeral. It occurred to him that there might be a connection between the two events, possibly one that would yield a novel. He remained at North Texas a week after graduation and wrote the first one hundred pages of *Horseman, Pass By*. By the fall of 1958, he had begun graduate work at Rice University and had completed the first draft of *Horseman* (between 1958 and 1961 he completed six drafts, more than he has done on any other book). According to McMurtry, the number of revisions indicated a "high degree of uncertainty about where the story lay, or how to write it. It was a dreadfully over-revised book. All the revising failed to make it less slight."[7] Although he made a number of revisions in this instance, McMurtry never rereads his work after it is in print. He told Mary Brinkerhoff of the *Dallas Morning News* (April 9, 1966) that "nothing is easier than to be detached from something you've written. By the time something gets between covers, one's emotion for it is completely exhausted . . . I'm cold as a stone on books I've already published." This statement parallels a similar one made a year later in *Collage;* when asked whether he preferred *The Last Picture Show* to *Leaving Cheyenne*, he replied ". . . it's hard for me to know because I've never read either one of them. I've only read them in the curious way one reads books while writing them" (*Collage,* May 1967, p. 7).

III   *Influence of the Beat Generation*

Not all of McMurtry's undergraduate writing perished in the flames with the fifty-two stories he burned. The short story "Roll, Jordan, Roll" appeared in the North Texas State University literary magazine, *Avesta,* in 1957. The same issue also carried his nonfiction article on the beat generation, "Journey to the End of the Road," an excellent piece of literary criticism, particularly since the beat writers had received very little critical attention by the time of its publication. The number of writers cited in the article attests to the fact that McMurtry had studied the beat movement from its beginning. Although he limits his discussion primarily to Jack Kerouac and Allen Ginsberg, he indicates Kenneth Rexroth's importance to the movement and traces the background of the beat generation. He concludes that "it takes no very astute eye to see that the San Francisco activity is in reality only the last and perhaps the most radical extension of an earlier 'Renaissance' which flourished in Chicago around 1915," and that the poets in San Francisco were not beat, "they're just the 'Neo-Lost.' " McMurtry points out that the identical pressures that moved the expatriates of the 1920's to Paris drove Kerouac and his companions giddily across the country to California (p. 34).

McMurtry's second critical appraisal of the beat movement, "The Beat Academy," appeared in the March 1960 issue of *Janus*, the Rice University literary magazine. By 1960, the movement had passed; it had thrived in the 1940's and had reached its zenith in 1957 when *On the Road* and "The White Negro" were published, "Howl" was confiscated, and McMurtry was assessing the movement in "Journey to the End of the Road." McMurtry's 1957 *Avesta* article, which begins "Let us rejoice—Bohemia has a seacoast at last," is primarily a discussion of the leading beat writers; the 1960 article is an attempt to break down "that unfortunate omnibus term, 'The Beat Generation,' " into practical components. The essay is also an attempt to "distinguish the Beat writer from the Beat loafer, the genuine from the phony, and the competent from the inept." McMurtry feels that the tendency to stir Ginsberg and Kerouac in the same pot with the "fragrant derelicts" of the movement is in part a result of the "Olympian negligence by *Time* punsters and run-down liberals in the *Partisan Review*":

Time, that esteemed journalistic organ some wag recently called "the weekly fiction magazine," takes a particular delight in bad-mouthing Beats, and has done all it can to see that the prevailing image is as stereotyped, though by no means as popular, as that of the TV cowboy. When *Time* can shame the poseurs of the movement into productive citizenry, or frighten them into the sea, then hurrah for *Time*; but until one or the other is accomplished some focusing distinctions need to be drawn. This essay, then, will be largely an attempt to clarify and proportion what the irresponsible national publicists have placed before us in a misemphasized and vaguely ominous lump. [P. 13]

The essay also traces briefly the two traditions behind the origins of the movement: the prevalence of the "little" magazine and the jazz movement of the 1940's, known as "Bop." Apparently, the major beat writers, particularly Kerouac, exerted an influence upon the young McMurtry; this influence is implicit in remarks he made in *Collage* in May 1967 and is also quite apparent in some of the pieces published in the *Coexistence Review* during his senior year at North Texas.

IV   The Coexistence Review: *Protest Poetry and Early
Variants of* Horseman, Pass By

Feeling stifled by the heavy-handed control and censorship
exerted over *Avesta*, the literary magazine officially sponsored by
North Texas State University, McMurtry and two other seniors at
the school decided to edit and publish *The Coexistence Review*. The
first issue caused the three editors to have difficulties with the
school administration. Although McMurtry had won a prize for a
poem to be published in *Avesta*, he had to withdraw the poem in the
wake of the controversy caused by the *Coexistence Review*, and,
according to fellow-editor Grover Lewis, the three editors later
learned that at one time school officials had seriously considered
expelling the three of them.

The first issue of the *Coexistence Review*, mimeographed on a
mottled gray paper, has a front cover depicting a six-pointed star—
outlined in red,—and a back cover depicting a stylized, crucified
Christ. The red color, the star, and the word *coexistence* in the title
contributed as much as the content to the controversy aroused by
the magazine's publication; the juxtaposition of communist and
Christian iconography was apparently unacceptable to school au-
thorities in the 1950's. This issue contains poetry of protest and
fragments from novels and novellas by the editors. At the bottom of
the first page is a list of the magazine's "spiritual advisers":
"Herschel Farrow, Bartholomew Vanzetti, James Agee, Dylan
Thomas, Thomas Wolfe, Charlie Parker, Garcia-Lorca, Miles Davis,
Lester Young, Django Reinhardt, Jean Genet, the Reverend Martin
Luther King, Jackson Pollock, the Hungarian Freedom Fighters,
Hart Crane, Charlie Chaplin, and the ghosts of the Lincoln
Brigade." At the top of the page is a poem, "Credo," by Larry
McMurtry:

Boo! you sanforized people.
you with TIME on your hands and LIFE on your ipana consciences.
you who hate NEGROES JEWS CATHOLICS NEIGHBORS VIRGINS POETRY
    TAXES & ANYTHING ELSE THAT LACKS UTILITY.
you who hid JESUS with other old easter eggs and beat your kids when they
    couldn't find HIM.
you who believe absolutely every word of scripture tv commercials the
    reader's digest dale carnegie billy graham and popular songs.
run on to your sleazy heaven and check the trade in on halos for me,
in case I can't find a flannel suit to match my SOUL.

The poem expresses the mood of the writers represented in this initial issue, which contains another McMurtry poem, "The Watch-Fires," as well as a fragment entitled " 'Grandad's End' A Section from *Horseman, Pass By.*" "The Watch-Fires" consists of four sections, titled "for James Agee," "for Lester Young," "for Hart Crane," and "for Erwin Smith."

"Grandad's End" is particularly interesting in its variance from the version finally printed in the novel. It depicts Lonnie's grandfather, Homer Bannon, "crawling, in his hurt and blindness and the summer-morning dark, down the road away from Headquarters; calling out to three lost phantoms from his ninety-year past: his dead son, Lucien; his foreman, Jericho Green, and Louisa, his first wife." In the novel Homer's first wife's name is Annie, the dead son's name is Dan, and the dialogue that follows is considerably different. There are more significant changes. In the *Coexistence Review* version, Homer Bannon is blind and senile; the Homer Bannon of the novel is active until the night of the accident. In the fragment, Lonnie and the ranch hand Jesse find Homer as they are driving back to the ranch with a truck load of horses; in the novel, Lonnie, who is driving a truck, and Hud, who is driving drunkenly behind with a woman in his Cadillac, discover Homer. In the novel, Hud kills the old man, and his motives for doing so are not entirely clear; Lonnie says, "I thought at first that he shot Granddad to stop the hurting. But seeing that wild blood-smeared grin, I didn't know. It could have been for kindness or for meanness either, whichever mood was on Hud when he held Granddad in the ditch" (p. 160). In the *Coexistence Review* version Jesse shoots the grandfather, and his act is explicitly one of euthanasia.

McMurtry cannot remember why he had Hud rather than Jesse kill the old man: "I have only the vaguest memory about that book because I completely killed myself on it by re-writing it so many times. I guess it was just a mistake to have Jesse do it in the first place. He would never have done it; it would have been out of character." When asked if he thought the killing is more consistent with Hud's character McMurtry said, "Well, it probably isn't, but it's closer. I never believed that, really; that was the bad thing about the novel. I feel very uncomfortable with it."[8]

On the cover of the second (and last) issue of the *Coexistence Review* is a loyalty oath signed by the three editors. The second page of this issue contains an editorial note explaining the unusual cover and also explaining some of the difficulties the young editors had undergone:

It has been brought rather forcibly to our attention that the first issue of *Coexistence Review* met with deep misunderstanding in several quarters. Apparently, the use of the word "coexistence," coupled with the color and design of the cover, and the generally iconoclastic tone of the material published, led a number of readers (if not buyers) of the initial edition to make assumptions and allegations that were not warranted. Let us hasten, then, in the face of this bigotry and lynch-spirit, to assure one and all that, as far as we are concerned, the *Coexistence Review* has been and will continue to be apolitical. Its sole purpose, in the beginning and in the present, is to disseminate to as wide an audience as possible the best creative work that we and our contributors are capable of producing. As novice artists, we are collectively and individually concerned with what Faulkner has termed "the old verities . . . of the heart"; none of us have time nor inclination for political polemic. Frankly, we just couldn't care less. To any who might wish to inquire further in this matter, we refer them to signed affidavits in the possession of the State of Texas, attesting to the effect that none of us is now or has ever been a member of any organization engaged in or advocating the overthrow of the U.S. government.

We wish to take this opportunity to offer our humble and abject apologies to those blameless and innocent persons who have suffered intimidation as a direct or indirect result of our publication; it is certainly our fervent wish that they may understand our original intentions in publishing *Coexistence Review*. To those others—all those who have great sloths filled with pustular fears and suspicions and hates—we offer all the pity and compassion we are able to summon up, and the cordial hope that they may sleep well. Amen.

The list of "spiritual advisers," which in the first issue is five lines in length, is extended to a full page in the second and is very much tongue-in-cheek.

The issue contains two poems by McMurtry. The first is "First Prize Winner*." The title has nothing to do with the poem; the asterisk refers to a footnote: "not long ago this poem was awarded first prize in a contest sponsored by a literary magazine now defunct." The reference is to the fact that the poem had won an *Avesta* prize but had to be withdrawn by McMurtry because of the trouble caused by the first issue of the *Coexistence Review*. The student editor of *Avesta* resigned in sympathy with McMurtry, a fact that accounts for the magazine's being "defunct" at the time McMurtry wrote the note. The second poem is entitled "from 'The Watch-

Fires,' for Jimmy Rodgers." This section does not appear among the fragments published in the first issue of the *Coexistence Review*. The second issue of the *Review* also contains prose fragments by McMurtry. "A fragment from Scarlet Ribbons," twenty lines of type about an idiot with smoke-grey eyes who sits on the floor of a bookstore and sings, was never developed. Later, McMurtry had forgotten that he had written it but recalled that the idiot in the sketch has no relation to the idiot Billy in *The Last Picture Show* but was the child of a Dallas bookshop proprietor. The model for Billy was a boy in McMurtry's hometown, Archer City.[9] The issue also contains a fragment, "from the Prologue to *Horseman, Pass By*" (four and a half pages of type), which differs somewhat from the prologue published in the novel and also from a third version published in *Southwest Review* (Spring 1961).

A note on the inside of the back cover indicates that because the editors were graduating seniors this was to be the last issue of the *Coexistence Review* published in Denton, but that it was hoped that the magazine could "establish editorial offices elsewhere, and continue to operate."

V *Postgraduate Experiences: Graduate School, Fellowships, and College Teaching*

After receiving the B.A. degree from North Texas State University, McMurtry established residency in Houston, Texas, where he began work toward a graduate degree in English at Rice University. He later utilized his graduate school experience at Rice and his subsequent tenure there after 1963 in *Moving On* (1970) and *All My Friends Are Going To Be Strangers* (1972). He obtained the M.A. degree from Rice University in 1960. In 1960 and 1961, he held a Wallace Stegner Fellowship at Stanford University. His California experience afforded material that he later utilized in his trilogy and will doubtlessly use in future novels. (In September 1972, McMurtry said that he was tired of Texas as a locale for his novels and that he felt that he now had enough "distance" to assimilate his California experience and to make it the subject for a "West Coast novel."[10]

McMurtry left California in 1961 to begin teaching at Texas Christian University in Fort Worth, where he taught during the 1961–1962 academic year. He did not teach the following year, however, for he was able to live on the money he received from the film *Hud*, the Paramount motion picture based on *Horseman, Pass By* (the film won three Academy Awards in 1963). He began teaching English and creative writing at Rice University (1963–1964) but was again relieved from his teaching duties when he received a Guggenheim award for creative writing (1964–1965). He resumed his teaching career at Rice University in 1965, and also began activity as a book scout and dealer for the Bookman, a Houston firm owned by Grace David.

VI   *Career As a Bookman*

McMurtry had exhibited a deep interest in books and book collecting before his affiliation with the Bookman. Although he grew up in what he describes as an "essentially bookless area," as a youth and later as a college student, he was an avid reader and book collector. As his collection grew, he found that he had made mistakes in his purchases and began selling volumes so that he could obtain more desirable titles or editions. While living in San Francisco during his association with the Stanford writers' workshop, he met a group of young book scouts, primarily poets or people associated with the periphery of the beat movement, who added to their meager livelihood by scouting for rare books, primarily rare modern titles, and selling them to specialist dealers. McMurtry began scouting himself and became quite proficient in ferreting out rare editions.

When McMurtry left Houston permanently to reside in Washington, D.C., he continued his interests in the book trade. After teaching briefly at George Mason College (spring semester, 1970) and at American University (1970–1971), he devoted all of his time to his writing and to Booked Up, a tiny rare-book shop nestled among the old Federal buildings in the Georgetown area of Washington. He considers book selling a "good balance to writing because it does not use any emotional energy; it is intellectual, and it is challenging to locate particular editions desired by people—to match the books to the collector."[11] McMurtry looks upon his activity in the book trade as an avocation or as a relaxation. "It is the opposite of writing," he said, "in that it is social and relaxing rather than introverting and solitary. I write in the morning and piddle around with the bookshop in the afternoon. The harder I work at writing, the more seriously I take it, the more concentration I give it, the more I realize I need a balance to it—that is, not simply myself sitting alone with a machine and concentrating all my energies upon creatures of fantasy."[12]

VII　*Early Essays and Book Reviews*

The early 1960's marked McMurtry's most active period as an essayist and reviewer. "The Beat Academy," which indicated that he was also a brilliantly incisive essayist, appeared in *Janus* in 1960. His "Notes on Vassar Miller," published in the same issue of *Janus*, is a brief but astute appraisal of Miller's poetry. In 1962, he began writing book reviews for the *Houston Post* and the *Saturday Review*. In general, McMurtry's book reviews are considerably less important than his other writing, and he is not enthusiastic about them: "I really have to strain to read Sunday-supplement reviews, of myself or anybody else. I had to strain to write them, too. The world's most leaden prose must appear in the bookpages of Sunday newspapers."[13]

McMurtry has also written essays on subjects other than literature. Those on Texas, indicating that he is no typical "Texian" who compulsively brags about his state, are particularly significant. In March 1966, the slick fashion magazine for men *Gentlemen's Quarterly* published a Texas issue, centering primarily on Dallas.[14] Along with feature articles on Dallas's haute cuisine and supper clubs, its "culture boom," and "the merchant prince and art patron, Stanley Marcus" was Larry McMurtry's "Dallas: A Reflection," in which he dissects the "Athens of the Alfalfa Fields." The article was truly the dissenting opinion in the issue. In it McMurtry says, "There is no place in Texas about which it is as hard to be generous, perhaps because there is no city in Texas where one finds so little generosity, so little openness of spirit" (p. 128). His attitude has nothing to do with the fact that President Kennedy was assassinated there:

I should say at once that I deplore the fashion of knocking Dallas because of the tragedy which happened there. The tragedy was the result of a private psychosis, not of the communal neurosis, the municipal malaise that afflicts Dallas; the farce that followed the tragedy was much more in character, much more Dallas. Nowadays, when I think of the city, the first image that springs to mind is a picture of Jack Ruby that hangs in a pawnshop window on Deep Elm, one of the state's most picturesque skid rows. It is a glossy picture of Ruby, taken in his glossy days: he is smiling, and his head is enfolded between the breasts of one of his strippers. . . . Jack Ruby is more symptomatic of the town than Dallas likes to think. He expresses a sort of psychic constriction that is fairly common in Dallas. . . . [P. 128]

McMurtry also attacks Dallas for being materialistic ("Dallas is clearly a money town") and for being conservative:

A shifting, confusing pattern of social and spiritual values is perhaps what lends Dallas conservatism its peculiar intensity and its hysteric tone. The conservative ladies' clubs are the most offensive and frightening part of this phenomenon, and their fervor seems really more religious than political. These old and not-so-old ladies have made super-patriotism a religious surrogate; they are true believers and they hate liberals in the way passionate religious dogmatists once hated heretics. Indeed, to the Dallas conservatives (and of course to many others) objectivity or truth is not the aim; conservative orthodoxy is the obvious aim, and perhaps the need for some convenient symbol of corruption which they can hate provides the real motivation. What would they do if they didn't have liberals to hate, if they didn't have *Lifeline* (the conservative radio show backed by Dallas' own H. L. Hunt) to stir them up and show them just how the Mistaken were ruining America? [P. 152]

Several months before the publication of the *Gentlemen's Quarterly* article, McMurtry's "Texas: Good Times Gone, or Here Again?" appeared in *Holiday* magazine (September 1965).[15] The article was primarily an attempt to reassess his attitudes about his state after traveling from its far southeastern corner (Brownsville) to its far northwestern corner (Texline)—a journey of almost fifteen hundred miles. This article deals essentially with small town and rural communities; it excludes the big cities of Houston and Dallas and the three principal cities of the Texas plain—Lubbock, Amarillo, and Wichita Falls—which McMurtry finds uniformly graceless and unattractive ("in summer they are hot and dry, in winter cold, dusty and windswept; the population is rigidly Protestant on the surface and underneath seethes with imperfectly repressed malice"). McMurtry states that there are few reasons why an imaginative person would stay in the small towns—"the brainy, the energetic, the imaginative, the beautiful—none of them can find much reason to stay" (p. 78).

In his investigation of the state McMurtry found the supplanting of rural and small-town traditions by urban and suburban traditions most interesting: "The folk—the people who have always lived on and worked the land—have lost their children to the city and the city's ways" (p. 58). This exodus resulted in a replacement of the frontier ethic with one better suited to life in the suburbs—"a people once severely ascetic has become almost sybaritic."

If Houston was left out of McMurtry's *Holiday* article on Texas, it was in for some oblique criticism in one he wrote on the city's Astrodome for the *Texas Observer*. Actually, McMurtry likes Houston, where he lived for six years; in an interview published in the *Houston Post* (October 30, 1966), he said, "I think Houston is getting better, better than almost any place other than New York, Los Angeles, or San Francisco." Nevertheless, he attacks the vulgarity of Houston's colossal sports stadium in "Love, Death, and the Astrodome" (*Texas Observer*, October 1, 1965). The article is full of wit and humor and reveals that McMurtry can be a gifted satirist when the occasion arises. For example, in speaking of the fancifully named skyboxes (the fifty-three costly and individually styled observatory-lounges), he notes such names as "Ramayana" and "Panjim Emerald," and says that he was a little disappointed that no one had thought of "Lingam Yoni."

His first view of the Astrodome was of its huge white dome "poked soothingly above the summer heat-haze like the working end of a gigantic rub-on deodorant" (p. 2). Apparently this was a case of form following function, he says, because when he asked why forty-five million dollars had been spent on such a structure, he was told it would keep Houston's sport fans from getting "so damp and sweaty." The explanation bothered McMurtry somewhat, for he has always been convinced that sports fans "deserve and perhaps require" the bad weather they get: "Braving frostbite and sunstroke helps keep their sadistic and masochistic tendencies in balance; when you make them more comfortable you may also make them meaner" (p. 3).

McMurtry is particularly humorous in his description of the tastelessness of the huge electronic scoreboard of the Houston Astrodome. But his humor is not always in so light a vein; often it blends with a serious social conviction:

Besides, pallid though the argument may appear, it seemed a bit conscienceless for a city with leprous slums, an inadequate charity hospital, a mediocre public library, a needy symphony, and other cultural and humanitarian deficiencies to sink more than $31 million in public funds into a ballpark. (Conscienceless, but not surprising. Houston is the kind of boom city that will endorse almost any amount of municipal vulgarity so long as it has a chance of making money. Here, it is customary to build in order to steal, and however questionable the motive, it means that all sorts of public marvels do get built). [P. 2]

Most of these early essays were subsequently incorporated in his first nonfiction book, *In a Narrow Grave*, a collection of essays on

Texas customs, beliefs, and cities. In this book—unlike his novels, which display a knowledge of and respect for the land—McMurtry reveals no sentimentality or nostaligia for the country, however descriptively he has written of it. In the *Houston Post* interview he says, "I like nature, but I still feel as if I am part of it, that I have never really separated from it, even in the city," But, he continues, he likes "bigger and better cities." This attitude, he says, separates his generation of Texas writers from older ones ("We don't seem to have this yen for the country and need of the country that Dobie, Bedichek and Webb had"). The big city's appeal to him is essentially cultural—theater, music, movies, art galleries—but it is also "a kind of emotional excitement that cannot be reduced to better theater, more music, better movies, and more book stores." This echoes the statement in his *Holiday* article (p78) and a similar idea that is fully developed in *The Last Picture Show*—that life in a small town can be hell after the last picture show closes. The town in *The Last Picture Show* is modeled on Archer City, about which McMurtry wrote, "Archer City is more isolated than when I lived there: the movie operates only intermittently, and the railroad tracks have been taken up" (*Holiday*, p. 77). McMurtry has written about life in the country and in the dead or dying little towns from firsthand experience. He told Arnold Rosenfeld, in the October 30, 1966 *Houston Post:*

"I think of my childhood as country, and my youth as small town. They aren't the same.

"In the country you depend on your family and your few neighbors, and you work things out in terms of your family and neighbors and an occasional hired hand and the animals.

"In a small town you have a more complex social life. There are more neighbors—real neighbors who live next door—schoolmates. Life becomes more complex. It tends to be generally confusing. It often contains more unsatisfactory elements—things that embarrass you, or humiliate you, or challenge you—than you had in the country." [P. 26]

In the interview in *Collage* he says that the broadest sociological theme underlying his fiction is that of the move away from the land—the homeplace. "I see country and city in opposition," he says, "offering different sorts of life possibilities, and I will probably go on writing for awhile about the people who are making the transition, or are about to make it" (pp. 7–8). His first two books, *Horse-*

man, *Pass By* and *Leaving Cheyenne*, are centered in the country, his third, *The Last Picture Show*, is about the small town, and his last three—*Moving On, All My Friends Are Going To Be Strangers*, and *Terms of Endearment*—are concerned with urban life.

CHAPTER 2

McMurtry's Novels

I Horseman, Pass By

THE action of McMurry's first novel, *Horseman, Pass By*, is filtered through the consciousness of Lonnie Bannon, who narrates the tightly structured story. Lonnie has lost both his parents and lives on a ranch with his grandfather, Homer Bannon, and his grandfather's nagging second wife. Honest, hard working, dignified, Homer Bannon epitomizes all the rugged virtues of a pioneer ethic. Now in his eighties, he represents a class of men who have virtually vanished with the frontier they helped to conquer. The old rancher sharply contrasts with his stepson, Hud, who is egotistic, ruthless, and totally unscrupulous in his pursuit of pleasure, be it sex, liquor, or money. Lonnie is caught between these two powerful polarities: the stoic pride and decency of his grandfather are awe inspiring, but Hud's hedonistic joy of life is equally fascinating. Other characters on the ranch also, though to a lesser degree, influence the formation of Lonnie's character. Jesse, the ranch hand and drifter, fills Lonnie with a longing for the open road, adventures in strange cities, and sexual experience; and Halmea, the Negro cook, senses his frustration and loneliness and becomes an understanding and sympathetic mother surrogate.

The catalyst for the action in the deceptively simple plot of the novel is the death of a heifer on the Bannon ranch. As Thomas Landess has pointed out, in the short fifteen-page first chapter, McMurtry introduces all the major characters and begins to develop the central action.[1] The death of the heifer is discussed casually in the kitchen of the Bannon ranch. Homer, mildly curious about the cause of death, states that he will call in the local veterinarian to examine the carcass. Characteristically, the callous and materialistic Hud objects, saying that the veterinarian is nothing but a "vaccine

28

salesman" who will use the death of the cow as an excuse to vacci-
nate the whole herd. "That's the stuff," says Hud. "Call in some
horse's ass to take your money. Don't never bother asking me what I
think about anything" (p. 11). He suggests that instead they sell the
still-warm carcass to a hide and rendering plant for soap. But Homer
persists in doing what he considers right for the good of his cattle; he
finds that the heifer died from the dreaded hoof-and-mouth disease,
and the entire herd must be destroyed. Landess correctly sees the
death of the cow as the event that precipitates the subsequent
tragedy of the Bannon ranch and leaves Lonnie rootless and alone to
face the vicissitudes of an unknown adulthood:

. . . by the end of the novel the lives of all have been changed by the death
of that one animal, and the tenuous communal ties that bind the ranch
together have been destroyed forever. Homer's spirit is broken when the
state veterinarian orders the herd destroyed, and the old man lives only
long enough to carry out his final responsibilities with dignity and precision.
Hud, who regards the protection of neighboring herds as a negligible responsibility, attempts to dissuade Homer from obeying the law, and failing,
tries to steal the ranch from him by legal chicanery. Lonnie, shocked into
manhood by a succession of tragedies which includes Hud's rape of Halmea
and mercy killing of Homer, decides to follow Jesse's example and "hit the
trail."[2]

The death of the cow also acts as a touchstone or index to the
characters of Homer and Hud. Homer is inevitably concerned with
the right and the ethical; Hud is characteristically concerned with
the expedient and lucrative. While the tests are being made to
determine the presence of hoof-and-mouth disease, Hud suggests
the hasty selling of the herd to an unsuspecting rancher. "I'll tell you
what I'd do," says Hud. "I'd get on the telephone tonight and sell
ever breed cow you got. They ain't got no chain on you yet, and we
could ship the old bitches out before you finish them tests" (p. 78).
Homer is scandalized at the suggestion of selling a contaminated
herd to "some old boy who wouldn't know what he was gettin,' "
and exclaims, "I'd have to be a whole lot worse off than I am to do
that" (p. 79). "Hell, no," continues Hud, "Sell 'em to someone
stupid enough to buy 'em knowing what the situation was. There's
many of 'em dumb enough to do it, just on the gamble." Homer,
however, remains adamant; "But that ain't no way to get out of a
tight" (p. 79). Homer's ethical behavior in this instance is so foolish

to Hud that he is convinced Homer is senile and determines to wrest control of the ranch from the old man through a power of attorney.

The real battle here, of course, is the conflict between the values of the old patrician rancher and the new "urbanized" cowboy personified by Hud. To Homer, the herd represents more than a livelihood; it is a way of life. For example, the state veterinarian attempts to console Homer by saying that he will be paid for the slaughter of his herd and that a year's quarantine on the ranch will be good for the grass. "It'll be just that much better for the herd you or these young men put on it," he says. "While it's empty you might sell a few oil leases or something. A ranch is more than just the cattle that's on it" (p. 105). Homer's reply expresses not only the agrarian ideal but his own deeply felt love for and identity with the land and the things that live on it:

"Oil," he said, looking down at his hands. "Maybe I could get some, but I don't believe I will. If there's oil down there these boys can get it sucked up after I'm under there with it. Something about this sickness, maybe I can't do much about, but the oil-field stuff I can. I don't like it an' I don't aim to have it. I guess I'm a queer, contrary old bastard, but there'll be no holes punched in this land while I'm here. They ain't gonna come in an' grade no roads, so the wind can blow me away." He looked up again, across the land. "What good's oil to me," he said. "What can I do with it? With a bunch of fuckin' oil wells. I can't ride out ever day an' prowl amongst 'em, like I can my cattle. I can't breed 'em or tend 'em, or chase 'em or nothin'. I can't feel a smidgen a pride in 'em, cause they ain't none my doin'. Money yes. Piss on that kinda money. I used to think it was all I was after, but I changed my mind. If I'd been in this business just for the money I'd a quit and started sellin' pencils or something back before you were born. I still like money as well as any man, nearly, and I done with it an' without it as much an' more than most people have, and I don't ever intend to let on I don't want a big share of it. But I want mine to come from something that keeps a man doing for himself." [pp. 105–106]

Thus, when Homer's magnificent herd of cattle is driven into pits to be slaughtered by rifle-firing government agents, the resultant carnage and death is more a personal than a financial loss to the old man. Looking down into the bloody pits after the firing ceases, Lonnie remarks, "Didn't take long." "Don't take very long to kill things," responds his grandfather. "Not like it takes to grow." (p. 126).

If Homer identifies with his cattle, he especially identifies with the two longhorn cattle that he has raised apart from the herd, neither to sell nor to slaughter but to symbolize his cattleman past. "I been keeping 'em to remind me how times was," he says. "Cattle like them make me feel like I'm in the cattle business" (p. 52). On the day his cattle are destroyed, Homer will not allow his ranch hand or the government agents to shoot the longhorns, but kills them himself in a symbolic execution of his past. When Lonnie finds his grandfather with the slain longhorns he thinks, "He might as well be dead with them, herd and herdsman together, in the dust with his cattle." (p. 129). Indeed, the destruction of the old man's herd has signalled the destruction of Homer himself; he goes rapidly into a physical and mental decline and is ultimately killed by his amoral stepson, Hud, when he is found critically injured on a ranch road.

Shocked by the death of his grandfather and by Hud's callous attitude, Lonnie leaves Thalia the day after Homer's funeral. Ostensibly he is going to Wichita to see his friend Hermy, who has been critically injured in a rodeo accident, but it is obvious that he does not plan to return for a long time. He withdraws all his money from the bank and hitches a ride with a friendly truck driver passing through Thalia on his way to New Mexico. As the truck speeds across the darkening prairie, Lonnie watches "the road and the big sky melt together in the north," and he is tempted to do as Jesse once suggested, to let the truck take him as far as it was going. The lonely restlessness Lonnie exhibits at the end of the novel heralds the aimless quests of the rootless males in McMurtry's later novels, *All My Friends Are Going To Be Strangers* and *Moving On*.

II Leaving Cheyenne

McMurtry's second novel, *Leaving Cheyenne*, was published in 1963. While not structured upon the theme of initiation, as is *Horseman, Pass By, Leaving Cheyenne* continues the motifs of loneliness and sense of loss found so abundantly in the first novel. The characters in *Leaving Cheyenne* are also bound to the town of Thalia and its immediate environs, the ranch country where they were born (the Cheyenne of the title is Thalia, but no one leaves it—except in death). McMurtry is not so much concerned with adolescence as he is with growing old, a motif continued in his next novel, *The Last Picture Show* (1966).

The plot of *Leaving Cheyenne* develops the triangular relationship that exists for almost half a century between the three main characters, Gideon Fry, Molly Taylor, and Johnny McCloud, a lifelong love that at first threatens their relationship but ultimately binds them together as they progress from youth to old age. McMurtry discussed his interest in the interactions of his characters in an interview published in *Collage* (May 1967, p. 8):

> In my work there are certainly patterns of isolation and attempts at connecting. . . . The most successful connections are in *Leaving Cheyenne*, which is also the book set most completely in the country. I was then and still am most interested in situations in which a person loves or is loved by more than one person. One man loves two women, one woman loves two men, etc. Such situations seem to me extremely rich for the novelist, rich in textural possibilities. I'm a great deal more sensitive to texture than I am to structure. I think, humanly, it's a very interesting question, how many people one can love.

Molly Taylor loves six men: her father; her husband, Eddie; her two lovers, Gid and Johnny; and her two sons. Molly's relationship with these men, particularly Gid and Johnny, so strongly dominates the action of the book that it might well have been titled *Molly*. The book is structured in four parts: the first section is Gid's narrative, the second Molly's, the third Johnny's, and the fourth the inscription on their tombstones. Both Gid and Johnny have loved Molly since they were boys, and the forty-six-year span of the book traces their strange relationship with her. The first and third sections reveal much about Molly; since she is the most important person in the lives of the two men, it is quite natural that their narratives are predominantly about her. Molly's own section, however, gives the reader the greatest insight into her personality. Although it deals with her memories of father, sons, and lovers, the section is really about her because in the account of her love for these men, Molly reveals that her life has been dedicated to unselfish giving. Gid's father, in a conversation with Molly, notes Molly's capacity for "giving," yet despite her unselfishness, she is fated to be lonely and unhappy, outliving her father, her husband, her sons, and her lover, Gid. The epigraph to her section (lines from Shakespeare's *Sonnet 64*) sums up her tragedy:

> Ruin has taught me thus to ruminate,
> That Time will come and take my Love away.

The first section of the novel, narrated by Gid, is concerned with the youthful years of the three lovers. Gid, who is twenty-one as his narrative begins, is a rival of his best friend, Johnny McCloud, for the love of Molly Taylor. Although Molly encourages Gid's sexual advances, she refuses to marry him, fearing that the relationship would destroy the deep friendship between Gid and Johnny, with whom she has also had sexual relations. Instead, she marries a callous oil-field worker, Eddie White. Shocked by Molly's action and by the suicide of his ailing father, Gid impetuously marries Mabel Peters, a cold and calculating woman whose frigidity markedly contrasts with Molly's warmth and passion just as Eddie's brutishness contrasts with Gid's sensitivity. Molly continues her relationship with Gid and Johnny after her marriage to Eddie, and has a son, Jimmy, by Gid, and another, Joe, by Johnny. Ultimately, Eddie is killed in an oil field accident. When she tells her sons the truth about their fathers, Joe, who has always loved Johnny, is delighted, but Jimmy, who has inherited Gid's puritanism, is shocked and never forgives Molly or Gid. Jimmy becomes a religious fanatic and, ultimately, a homosexual.

Section two, narrated by Molly, relates the middle years of the intertwined lives of Gid, Johnny, and Molly. She continues the sexual relationships with Gid and Johnny but steadfastly refuses to marry Gid, whose marriage with Mabel has become a shambles. Although she has always loved Gid "the most," she still thinks that to marry him would be detrimental to his happiness. When her two sons are killed in World War II, Gid, who feels that their son Jimmy's death is a judgment on them, refuses to sleep with Molly any longer. The cessation of their lovemaking is as painful to Molly as it is to Gid, but she respects him too much to try to dissuade him from doing what he considers right.

Johnny narrates the third section of the book, which focuses primarily on Gid's declining health, and, finally, his death. It is a section replete with reminiscence and nostalgia on the part of the aging trio. The tone of Johnny's section is elegiac, stressing the cyclic nature of life. It is the most poignant writing McMurtry has ever done and, without being maudlin, prepares the reader for an acceptance of the finitude of love and life, symbolized by the fourth section of the book: the inscription on the tombstones of the three old friends.

Despite the critical consensus that *Leaving Cheyenne* is McMurtry's best novel, McMurtry himself seems to have become a little embarrassed by it as he has matured. In this context the remarks he made in May 1967 in the *Collage* interview (p. 8) afford an interesting contrast to the attitude he takes toward the novel in an article published in *New York* magazine, April 1974.

As for *Leaving Cheyenne*, evidently the most admired of my novels, I wish I could still love it but I don't. It is perhaps worth pointing out that both it and my first novel were written in the same year—my twenty-third. I revised around on both books for a while, but essentially both incorporate, at best, a 22-year-old's vision. I wish I had the audacity, not to mention the energy, to write two novels a year now, but I don't want that vision back, nor am I overjoyed to see the literary results of it applauded. *Leaving Cheyenne* is a lifelong triangle—two men and a woman who go on loving and sharing one another for forty years. I was fond of it when I finished it, and for a number of years thereafter, but as emotion cooled and memory dimmed I came to notice that the people who admired the book most extravagantly all seemed to be male journalists. That was a circumstance too provocative to be ignored. I don't believe I know a class of people who are as clearly the captives of their own fantasies as the male journalists among my acquaintances, and it slowly became evident to me that *Leaving Cheyenne* had happened to express, with all the convincingness of 22, a primary male-journalist fantasy: that of being able to sleep with one's best friend's wife or girl friend without there being any hard feelings on the part of the best friend. What *Leaving Cheyenne* really offers is a vision of adult life in which sexuality cannot seriously interfere with friendship—little wonder people adore it.[3]

III   The Last Picture Show

In *The Last Picture Show*, McMurtry moves from the bare plains and isolated ranches that were the setting of *Horseman, Pass By* and *Leaving Cheyenne* to the spiritually stifling confines of Thalia, a west Texas oil town. He examines the town's inhabitants—the oil rich, the roughnecks, the religious fanatics, the high school football stars, the love-starved women,—with an eye that is at once sociological and satiric. For the first time he abandons the first-person narrative in his fiction, and the result is a dispassionate, cold look at the sordidness and hypocrisy that characterize the town. The action centers around the sexual adventures and misadventures of Sonny Crawford as he struggles toward maturity in the emotionally crippling environs of Thalia. Sonny's mother dies when he is quite young, and his father, a drug addict, can provide him with no masculine model to emulate. Sonny lives in a cheap rooming house with his friend Duane, who is also essentially parentless (his father is dead and his working mother has virtually abandoned him). The surrogate parents for the two adolescents are Sam the Lion, owner of the local pool hall, café, and movie house, and Genevieve, a waitress in Sam's café who watches over the boys' meals and listens to their problems with motherly concern and affection.

Both boys are enamored of the same girl, a situation somewhat analogous to Gid and Johnny's mutual love for Molly in *Leaving Cheyenne*. The object of their affection, however, Jacy Farrow, is the antithesis of Molly. The spoiled only child of an oil-rich ex-roughneck, Jacy is narcissistic and selfish. Her moral depravity and promiscuity are encouraged by the cynical counsel of her amoral mother, Lois. Read strictly on the literal level, *The Last Picture Show* describes a Peyton Place on the prairie, for the plot abounds in many scatalogical scenes that are explicit and often perverse in running the full gamut of small-town sexuality, including masturbation, exhibitionism, adultery, zoophilia, and group sex. This aspect of the book is epitomized by Lois Farrow, who, after having sexual relations with Sonny on the night of his abortive marriage to her daughter, Jacy, says: "Your mother and I sat next to one another in the first grade. We graduated together. I sure didn't expect to sleep with her son. That's small town life for you" (p. 255). Such comments, however, must be examined in the context of the general tone of the book, which employs not only ironic satire but also much black humor. The ironic tone of the book is sustained from the dedication ("lovingly dedicated to my home town") to the final chapter and is underscored by McMurtry's use of black humor, as the names of some of his characters suggest.

The plot of *The Last Picture Show* is concerned with the rites of passage of Sonny Crawford and his friend, Duane Jackson. Both boys are high school seniors and co-captains of the town's football team. Sonny and Duane spend most of their time at the pool hall, the all-night café, or the movie house, all owned by Sam the Lion. When Sonny terminates his relationship with his "steady" girl, Charlene Duggs, he begins an affair with Ruth Popper, the neglected wife of the high school coach. Sonny responds to Ruth's loneliness, and she fulfills Sonny's need for sex and affection. Sonny is temporarily banned from the pool hall, café, and movie house when Sam the Lion learns of his involvement with the sexual initiation of the half-witted boy, Billy. Sonny's banishment has serious psychological implications, for not only is Sam the Lion a father figure to Sonny, but his café, pool hall, and movie house are places of refuge for the homeless and essentially parentless boy. Sonny's isolation is subsequently intensified with the death of Sam the Lion and his estrangement from Ruth Popper by the actions of Jacy, who, out of pique and boredom, seduces Sonny from the aging Ruth. Sonny's relations with Jacy also cause his friend Duane to become jealous and, in a fight with Duane, Sonny is blinded in one eye. As a lark, the spoiled and egocentric Jacy marries Sonny but, as she anticipates, her parents have the marriage annulled before it is consummated. Jacy leaves town to attend college, Duane leaves for the war in Korea, the movie house closes, and Billy is struck down and killed by a truck. Bereft of friends, father figure, and emotional release via the picture shows, Sonny drives to the edge of town in a futile attempt to escape from the confines of the stultifying and moribund little town but realizes that he has no place to go. He returns to Ruth who, after a brief but bitter condemnation of his betrayal, takes him back. "What if he had valued a silly young girl more than her? It was only stupid, only the sort of thing a boy would do," she thinks (p. 279). Ruth rationalizes that the pain he has caused her is not important and that because they had both suffered, she could now teach him the meaning of life.

McMurtry's characterization is not as successful in *The Last Picture Show* as it is in the first two novels. As Thomas Landess has pointed out, despite the credibility of Sonny, Duane, and Ruth Popper, the characterizations are often sterotypic: Jacy is the spoiled rich girl, Brother Blanton the fundamentalist preacher, Genevieve the good-hearted working girl, Billy the sublime idiot.[4] The stereotypic even verges on caricature in the characterization of Coach Popper, the hairy-chested football coach who is a latent homosexual. There are subtle nuances in the characterization of Genevieve, however, who, along with Sam the Lion, provides a moral arbiter for the boys. She (and Ruth Popper) is one of McMurtry's many mature women who play such an important role in the sophistication or maturing process of his young male protagonists. Abilene belongs to the category of ruthless, sensual amoralists established by Hud in *Horseman, Pass By*, and anticipates the less extreme avatar of the type seen in Sonny Shanks in *Moving On* (1970). Sam the Lion represents the type of mature male figure, which also includes Homer Bannon in *Horseman, Pass By* and Adam Fry in *Leaving Cheyenne*.

IV *The Urban Trilogy*

McMurtry's first three novels concerned individuals closely connected with the land or with the immediate confines of their village environment. These works are essentially regional novels, for although they contain undeniably universal themes, the actions of the characters are determined by the cultural tradition of west Texas, both in its rural and small-town contexts. The first three novels are also somewhat autobiographical in that they represent McMurtry's own ambivalent attitudes about his region. McMurtry considered his childhood "country" and his youth "small town." In the country, life was simpler; one depended on his family and few neighbors, an occasional hired hand, and the animals. In the small town, life became "more complex" and "confusing" with factors that "challenged, embarrassed, or humiliated" the individual.[5] McMurtry's young manhood was spent in the city, and this experience is utilized in the urban trilogy: *Moving On* (1970), *All My Friends Are Going To Be Strangers* (1972), and *Terms of Endearment* (1975).

McMurtry said that from their "moment of conception," these three books had been projected as a trilogy, although he was not quite sure of the direction the books would take. The trilogy itself was only "vaguely conceived in the sense that I did not know the whole design and still don't [at the time of writing the third novel]."

I set out to write a book about Patsy, thinking it was going to be a trilogy; then I did the Danny book, and I began to see what I was working with was three different types of young people: Danny, Patsy, and Emma. I was somewhat surprised to see how Emma's mother took over in such a major way in the third novel, although I think it is good she did—I think another novel about those same people in Houston would be boring if there were not some real alteration of perspective. The whole portion of time that is covered in *Moving On* is seen in this novel from Emma's mother's point of view, rather than Emma's, and so you don't have a sense of repeating all these events from another young person's point of view. In a sense, however, the central theme is still there; Emma caught between Patsy and Danny, in a way. It's not that different from *Leaving Cheyenne*, really; there's something of the same: three people, three times, three styles.[6]

McMurtry's method of composing his trilogy is curious: the first book published, *Moving On* (1970), was originally intended to be the last in the series. The second book published, *All My Friends Are Going To Be Strangers* (1972), is the first book of the trilogy. The third novel in the epic to be published, *Terms of Endearment*

(1975), was to be the middle, or second, in the series. As originally conceived, the order of composition represented a reversal of the old epic formula; McMurtry was to end, rather than begin, in *media res*. By the fall of 1972, however, with less than half of the third novel completed, McMurtry said that this final volume would overlap both of the earlier novels, beginning on the weekend where Danny attends the abortive autograph party for his book in Houston (*All My Friends Are Going To Be Strangers*, chapter 16) and extending beyond the period covered in *Moving On* by about ten years. McMurtry does not intend to write Faulknerian epics or a Southwestern Yoknapatawpha saga, although he does like "connected novels." He has already written a trilogy, and he has suggested that his next novels will be set in California and might be "tangentially" connected to some of the characters in the urban trilogy (for instance, Jill in *All My Friends Are Going To Be Strangers*).[7]

V Moving On

The plot of *Moving On* focuses on the disintegration of the marriage of Patsy and Jim Carpenter. Although primarily concerned with Patsy's emotional growth, *Moving On* also contains insights into contemporary Southwestern life: the oil and ranching rich, the professional rodeo set, the university graduate students, and the lower-income group of Southeast Houston. The novel is long (794 pages) and contains numerous subplots and characters, among them, the world championship rodeo star, Sonny Shanks, and his mistress, the ranching heiress Eleanor Guthrie; the rodeo clown Pete Tatum and his young barrel-racing wife, Boots; the philandering college professor, Bill Duffin, and his cynical, frustrated wife, Lee; the struggling graduate student, Flap Horton, and his placid wife, Emma; Jim's fellow graduate student, Hank Malory, and his mistress, Clara Clark; Jim's aging uncle, the rancher Roger Waggoner; and Patsy's sister Miri, a pregnant and unmarried hippie dropout.

McMurtry manages to thread the actions of all these characters into the life of Patsy Carpenter, and each is contributory to her gradually awakening self-awareness. Sonny Shanks's aggressive sexuality, for instance, polarizes the quiet, sad admiration that Pete Tatum has for Patsy. Pete, like Pee Wee Baskin, unable to articulate the adoration he feels for her, must worship her in silence. The attitudes of all three men are in contrast to that of her callow husband and make Patsy feel desirable at a time when he is neglecting her. Patsy's brief encounter with the aging heiress, Eleanor Guthrie, increases her own sophistication by offering a worthy feminine model to emulate. Despite her immense wealth, Eleanor expects little happiness in life. Her inner strength and quiet dignity is in marked contrast to the caustic neuroticism of Lee Duffin. Acting in counterpoint to the extremes of stoicism and pessimism represented by these older women, Patsy's fat and amiable friend Emma Horton is a good and simple-natured earth mother who serves as confidante and sounding board for Patsy's many problems and moods. Ultimately, however, Patsy realizes that the marriage of Emma and Flap Horton, like her own and that of the Duffins, is a failure. Patsy wants neither the vacuousness of the Horton's marriage nor the hostility of the Duffins', and in desperation she seeks an outlet from her own empty marriage in a friend and classmate of her husband, Hank Malory.

Hank represents a mean between the two extremes of Patsy's other admirers, Sonny Shanks and Pete Tatum; he has both Pete's sad, silent quality and Sonny's insatiable sexual appetite. He easily seduces Patsy and proves to be an ardent lover. The affair with Hank, however, is mere lust, not love, for although Hank thinks he is in love with Patsy, he is really consumed by a desire that blinds any realization of her as an individual. "He had stopped seeing her, and only wanted her; his fumblings were impersonal and crude" (p. 323); "all he felt was impatience and desire, things he had felt almost from the first time he had seen her. Her objections didn't register with him; he wanted her too much" (p. 344); "The minute he really began to want her he stopped seeing her—it had been that way even the first day. He ceased to be the man she was so fond of, so comfortable with, and just became a man, thrusting himself at her so strongly that it was scary" (pp. 344–345); "He really noted nothing except her body—it was her body he knew, not her" (p. 556).

Hank's desire is at first a welcome catharsis for Patsy: "His own desire was blind—it was for her, but it took little account of her, except as a body, and once she got over being shaken by it she found she liked it that way. . . . Once she relaxed and accepted the new terms on which she was desired, she began to respond, and soon responded more strongly than she ever had" (p. 444). She needed to be desired and to have desire awakened in her. Ultimately, however, Patsy realizes that the relationship they have is not love, and she tells Hank, "Maybe I was just desperate for someone to want me the way you do" (p. 557).

If her affair with Hank frees Patsy emotionally from a passionless relationship with Jim, it also frees her physically from her unsatisfactory marriage. When Jim discovers the affair, he leaves for California with another graduate student, Hank's former mistress, Clara Clark. Jim's departure signals the breakup of Patsy's marriage.

Unlike *Horseman, Pass By, The Last Picture Show,* and *All My Friends Are Going To Be Strangers,* which have young males as protagonists, *Moving On* concentrates on the rites of passage of Patsy Carpenter: at the novel's end, Patsy cries less, is less selfish and self-pitying, and looks forward with some optimism to a new, emancipated life. Although the novel is ostensibly about Patsy, the primary concern is modern marriage, for Patsy's marriage is not the only one that is unhappy. The subplots of this lengthy novel abound in failing or failed marriages: Eleanor Guthrie was formerly married to a homosexual who committed suicide; Pete Tatum's first wife was unfaithful to him, and his second marriage forces him to lead a miserable life as a car salesman; Bill and Lee Duffin cling tenuously to a marriage blemished by hostility and infidelity; Patsy's parents, Garland and Jeanette White, have a dull relationship; and Emma's love is not enough to keep Flap happy or from attempting suicide. *Moving On* is McMurtry's longest treatment of the failure of marriage, an omnipresent theme in his fiction.

Moving On, written over a long period of time, went through many radical revisions. The editorial correspondence concerning the novel and its many early drafts indicate the difficulty McMurtry had in finding a direction for his book.[8] Even the various titles given to early drafts of the novel testify to McMurtry's uncertainty about the direction of the narrative. (McMurtry thinks that his titles were important in determining the direction his novels took.)[9] A May 25, 1964, letter from McMurtry's editor, John Leggett, refers to *Sometimes the Matador,* obviously an early draft of *Moving On.* Leggett objected to the title "because it suggests bullfighting" (the remainder tables are "groaning" with matadors and corridas, he notes). A few months later, Leggett objected to the episodic aspects of the novel (now called *Lovebreaking*) and the changes in location of the action: "You have no idea what intensity you lose (particularly in going to California) by flouting the unities—nor what you stand to gain here by staying in the arena, and the bars and cars and trailers around it and by keeping the elapsed time to a minimum—flashing back when its absolutely necessary.[10]

At this time, according to McMurtry, he was working on a novel "about a boy from a West Texas small town making his way to Hollywood, to the fringe of the world of movie-extras and TV Westerns—and since he gets there via the world of professional rodeo it will probably be advertised as a rodeo novel. However, rodeo is only its context, and its principal concern is the confusion and anxiety—marital, sexual, and otherwise—which this kind of dislocation can cause."[11] The novel also went through a version that was given as the working title *The Water and the Blood*.[12] In this version, the novel is told in the first person by a series of narrators. Hank, Patsy, and Pete each have their own sections that they narrate, utilizing the narrative technique employed in *Leaving Cheyenne*. McMurtry abandoned this technique in the final version of the novel, which utilizes the third person omniscient point of view.

VI All My Friends Are Going To Be Strangers

Narrated in the first person by a young, naive graduate student, Danny Deck, *All My Friends Are Going To Be Strangers* recounts the amorous adventures of the protagonist on an extended journey from Texas to California and back to Texas again. The plot of the novel is episodic, and the characters are myriad. The minor ones include editors, authors, movie producers, professors, students, librarians, janitors, cowboys, and Texas Rangers. The main ones are primarily women who are sexually involved with Danny at one time or another: Sally Bynum, Jenny Salomea, Emma Horton, Jill Peel (he also has brief sexual encounters with two minor female characters, Juanita, a Mexican whore, and a novelist, Renata Morris).

Danny, a graduate student at Rice University in Houston, Texas, meets Sally Bynum at a party given by a university professor in Austin, falls in love with her immediately, and a week later impetuously marries her. The marriage seems doomed to dissolution from the beginning, for Sally wants only to have a baby and soon withdraws into herself. After Danny's first novel is accepted for publication, the couple move to California, and the trip to San Francisco marks the final break up of their marriage. Sally discovers that she is pregnant in California and acquires two lovers there before returning to Houston to have her baby. Danny moves out of their apart-

ment after he discovers her first affair. He makes a brief trip to Los
Angeles to work on the movie adaptation of his book, and while in
Hollywood has a brief affair with a novelist, Renata Morris. He then
meets a strange and lovely artist, Jill Peel, whom he takes back to
San Francisco to live briefly with him in an almost idyllic relation-
ship made up of discussions of literature and art.

Danny falls in love with Jill, who proves to be deeply disturbed
and incapable of giving herself freely in sex. When Jill leaves for
New York on an assignment, the lonely and frustrated Danny returns to Texas to see his child and to attend an autograph party to
promote his book in Houston. On his way back, he visits his great-
uncle, Laredo, a mad west Texas rancher who, after eighty-nine
years of bachelorhood, made an unhappy marriage with a woman on
a neighboring ranch. Upon his arrival in Houston, Danny is pre-
vented from seeing his newborn child by the intervention of Sally's
parents. The autograph party also fails when no one comes to the
bookstore. In a depressed and lonely state, Danny makes love to a
rich neighbor, Jenny Salomea, and to Emma Horton, the wife of a
fellow graduate student. He then leaves Houston with Petey, a
Mexican janitor from the school library. After a disastrous encounter
with two Texas Rangers, Petey is arrested and Danny is badly
beaten. He proceeds to McAllen, Texas, crosses the Mexican bor-
der, and spends some time with Juanita, a Mexican whore. When
she compliments Danny, he impulsively asks her to return to the
United States with him, but Juanita wisely refuses, and Danny continues his aimless trek. He talks briefly to a retired motion picture
actor who tries to give him sage advice, but Danny is beyond recon-
ciliation with the world and with himself. At the end of the book, he
wades into the Rio Grande River, walking toward Mexico. When he
is midstream, he "drowns" the manuscript of his second novel,
holding the pages under the surface until they sink. The novel ends
with Danny, exhausted and intoxicated by liquor and hallucinatory
mushrooms, wading deeper into the water, thinking of Jill and his
lost opportunity.

McMurtry, of course, was himself a graduate student in Houston,
and, like Danny, he spent some time in San Francisco. Doubtlessly
he drew upon his California experience in writing *All My Friends
Are Going To Be Strangers*, particularly in his spoofing of literary
parties and the Keseyite trippers (part of the dedication of McMurtry's *In a Narrow Grave* is "for Ken Kesey, the last wagon-master").

McMurtry says, however, that the only autobiographical part of the book is the protagonist's questioning whether writing is destructive. McMurtry feels that he has been much concerned with this question and is convinced that in the larger sense writing is self-destructive and that it is "a tricky thing to manage throughout a lifetime":

It is true that the better you write the worse you live. The more of yourself you take out of real relationships and project into fantasy relationship the more the real relationships suffer. The popular theory is that writing grows out of a neurosis, and is a cure for neurosis. This is nonsense. It may grow out of the neurosis, but it doesn't cure it; if anything, it drives it deeper and makes it nearer to being a psychosis. I do not think that *real* writing is a purgative, though there must be some people who let off tensions by writing. I do not think that writing, or any art, pursued seriously, is necessarily a health producing activity. Writing involves a kind of gambling with the subconscious and the destruction of self-defenses. I don't encourage young people to write, for several reasons. For one thing, it's a very difficult profession. Not very many of them could conceivably make a living at it; not very many of them could conceivably have a very satisfactory life—unless they are geniuses, and then they don't need advice from anybody. I'm just not sure that it is a health-producing or joy-producing activity.[13]

Addressing his remarks specifically to the character of Danny Deck, McMurtry says, "Danny is aware of all this as a problem—that there is some relationship between writing and life, and that it is not clear-cut. He has some sense at the end of the book that it is hopeless, that either he won't be much of a writer, or that the better he writes, somehow, the more it's going to alienate him. And I don't know but what I believe that, at least I think it's desirable."[14]

Danny Deck disappears from the chronology of the trilogy by wading into the river at the end of *All My Friends Are Going To Be Strangers*. There is an ambiguity at the end of the novel because the reader can only hypothesize what finally becomes of Danny. McMurtry left the ending ambiguous because he really does not know what happens to the protagonist. On the question of whether Danny commits suicide, McMurtry says:

Danny is not suicidal, although he has passed through an emotional recognition which is in a sense suicidal. On the other hand, he might well drown, because he has been floundering around for four or five days without sleep, and is high, and is very confused. His intentions are to go to Mexico, but I have never really decided in my mind. Except that he never reappears.

That is taken care of at the end of *Moving On*—he has officially disappeared and has never been seen again. He reappears in the novel I am writing now, but this novel overlaps. It starts on the weekend when he comes to Houston for his autograph party, and carries over beyond *Moving On* for about ten more years, but we see no more of Danny than we've seen of him in *All My Friends*—we just see him in the very first section of the novel—and the night he spends with Emma.[15]

VII   Terms of Endearment

The final volume in McMurtry's urban trilogy, *Terms of Endearment*, concentrates on the eccentric mother of Emma Horton, Aurora Greenway. Aurora, a forty-nine year old widowed New Englander, has ensconced herself in a Spanish colonial style house in Houston from which she exerts a subtle tyranny upon her entourage of suitors, her daughter, Emma, and her maid, Rosie. Part madcap, part Circe, Aurora is a combination Auntie Mame and Semiramis, and few men fail to respond to the charms of the aging beauty. Her suitors include General Hector Scott, an almost parodic characterization of the stiff-backed military type; Edward, a bashful and bumbling banker; Trevor, a suave yachtsman; Alberto, an aging, retired opera singer, and Vernon, a millionaire oilman who lives in the back seat of his customized Lincoln.

The novel is divided into two books. Book I, "Emma's Mother 1962," is couched in a style characteristic of a comedy of manners. The social comedy and satire of book I is brilliant, but there is a departure from the overall light tone in chapter 13, where there is a return to the black humor and caricature reminiscent of *The Last Picture Show*, although it is less subtly handled. This chapter, concerned with a jealous husband who chases his wife across a honky-tonk dance floor in a potato-chip truck, originally appeared in *Playboy* and constitutes a jarring note in the context of the rest of Book I.[16]

But if chapter 13 seems out of place in the narrative of the amusing adventures of Aurora Greenway, Book II, "Mrs. Greenway's Daughter, 1971–1976," seems an unfortuitous addendum to the novel. Book I is comprised of nineteen chapters and is 360 pages in length. Book II contains only one chapter, forty-seven pages long. This imbalance in structure is intensified by both the style and content of the second book: Book I is a leisurely glance at one year in the life of Emma's mother; Book II attempts to capsulate five years in Emma's life, including the final deterioration of her marriage, two doomed love affairs, and her lengthy and tragic death from cancer. In a series of scenes, various characters from Book I, Emma's mother, her children, her friends, come to the hospital room of the dying Emma. Many of the scenes, particularly those in which she bids farewell to her children, are needlessly maudlin, and the general melodrama of Book II is totally out of keeping with the light satire and comedy of Book I.

Viewed in whole or in part, *Terms of Endearment* constitutes a departure from the theme established in the other two novels in the trilogy. *All My Friends Are Going To Be Strangers* and *Moving On* deal with the confusion and disassociation wrought upon people who are uprooted from the land and its traditions and who are placed in an impersonal urban setting. Janis P. Stout observes that "none of the characters in these two novels has any sense of a usable past, and none is purposefully directed toward the future. They inhabit the burgeoning cities of Texas with no apparent means of orienting themselves and nothing to engage them but endless, unsatisfying motion—as the title *Moving On* well indicates."[17] On the other hand, the greater portion of *Terms of Endearment* focuses on an East Coast widow who is perfectly acclimated to life in the sprawling urban environment of Houston. The only real linking device of thematic significance between *Terms of Endearment* and the first two novels of the trilogy is in the story of Emma, certainly a minor character in Book I, albeit the protagonist of the rather arbitrarily appended Book II. In Book II, Emma and her husband move from Flap's graduate school in Houston to a series of teaching assignments in the Midwest, and, as in the two earlier novels, it becomes obvious that "university life is a way-station for academic migrants and those who have not yet decided where they want to go."[18] Indeed, Flap's peregrinations from one faculty post to another traces the inevitable erosion of their marriage. The marriage motif has the greatest continuity of theme not only with the first two novels in the trilogy but also with McMurtry's other three novels, for the theme of the dissolution of marriage permeates McMurtry's entire canon. Emma and Flap Horton's marriage is precarious in *Moving On* and in *All My Friends Are Going To Be Strangers* and fails completely in *Terms of Endearment*, which begins with a discussion of marriage between Emma and Aurora Greenway.

CHAPTER 3

Major Themes in McMurtry's Fiction

I Initiation

Mc MURTRY'S first three novels—*Horseman, Pass By, Leaving Cheyenne,* and *The Last Picture Show*—can be analyzed as initiation novels, for all involve the introduction of the protagonist to the meaning of life through its two universal paradigms: love (sex) and death. Lonnie, in *Horseman, Pass By,* is driven from his childhood environment by several initiatory shocks involving love and death—all of them violent. Troubled by his own awakening sexuality, Lonnie must experience the brutal rape of his love object and mother surrogate, Halmea, and the killing of his grandfather, Homer. Similarly, Gid, in *Leaving Cheyenne,* must undergo the traumatic loss of Molly to another man, the suicide of his father, and the estrangement and death of his son, Jimmy. Sonny, in *The Last Picture Show,* must be frustrated in his desire for Jacy, lose an eye for her, and lose his friend Billy and his father surrogate Sam through sudden and unexpected death.

In the beginning of *Horseman, Pass By,* Lonnie's expressions of discontent and restlessness are symptomatic of his awakening sexuality, catalyzed by the presence of the brown-skinned Halmea on his grandfather's ranch. Halmea is more aware of Lonnie's problem than he is, revealed in the incident in which she goodnaturedly refuses to go fishing with him. Halmea is the only woman on the ranch besides Lonnie's grandmother, and Lonnie constantly thinks of Halmea's melon-shaped breasts (even at his grandfather's funeral, he notes that he likes "the rich brown wood of the church seats, wood that was the color of Halmea's breasts"). The primary motivation for Lon's wanting to escape the confines of the ranch, of Thalia itself, is to discover himself through sexual experience:" I lay awake in bed with my eyes open, thinking about all the girls I knew in

46

Thalia, and those in Oklahoma City I didn't know, all of them with nightgowns on, asleep somewhere and breathing in the night" (p. 58).

Neither Updike nor Salinger has been as successful as McMurtry in describing the gnawing ache that accompanies adolescent sexuality. It is this same awakening sexuality that racks the boys in *The Last Picture Show*. Sex dominates their thoughts and their conversations, and it is the motivation for many of their actions (both foolish and violent). Lonnie's own struggle with his pent-up emotions (it should be compared with that of the townboy, Marlet) is most intense in chapter 7: "My room didn't do much to cheer me up. I read in about half a dozen books, but I couldn't get interested in any of them, and I finally fished out a couple old *Playboys* and went through them, looking at the shiny, naked girls. But whatever I did, that night, I just seemed to get more and more restless; it was like an itch there's no way to scratch." (p. 85). Finally, late in the night, he dresses, gets a flashlight, a rifle, and a box of shells and goes out into the dark. "I decided to go shoot things, shoot anything I could find," he says. And he does—some dozen frogs, a turtle, a rabbit. "Tonight I may shoot everything," he thinks. After the slaughter at the water tank he feels, like Marlet, as if he is strangling. He runs cold water over his body, then goes to Halmea's cabin, where he finds sympathy and understanding. Halmea tells him, "You had de blues about sometin', I seen dat at suppah . . . . You got mo' kinks in you dan I got in my back."

Halmea understands men, and she understands the adolescent male—she knows how sex can drive a man, causing him to be clownish, lovable, or vicious. She has been amused by Lon's sexual awakening, by his obvious and bungling overtures; now she can sympathize with his frustration and anxiety. She somewhat parallels Molly in *Leaving Cheyenne*, who realizes the importance of sex to a man: "It was because a man needed it, and had it all tangled up with his pride" (p. 201). Indeed, it is only with the magnificently realized character of Molly that any of McMurtry's males find happiness, fleeting though it may be. Lonnie, in *Horseman, Pass By*, remains unfulfilled, and in the epilogue, it is apparent that he must flee Thalia and its environs ("to lean back and let the truck take me as far as it was going"). But he is going only as far as nearby Wichita, where his friend is hospitalized. He was correct when he sensed the futility for himself and his friends: "All of them wanted more and seemed to end up with less; they wanted excitement and ended up stomped by a bull or smashed against a highway; or they wanted a girl to court; and anyway, whatever it was they wanted, that was what they ended up doing without."

Thomas Landess argues that Jesse provides Lonnie with an immediate example to follow at the end of the narrative. Lonnie "takes to the road," writes Landess, "presumably to endure the loneliness and hard knocks that life has to offer. And he makes this choice despite Jesse's warning that Homer Bannon is the better model for emulation."[1] Lonnie, however, is under no illusions about what he will find at the end of the road, but with his grandfather dead, Halmea gone, and Hud in apparent control of the ranch, he determines to leave the place of his roots. Indeed, Lonnie seems destined to pursue the endless quest of the protagonists in McMurty's road novels, *Moving On* (1970) and *All My Friends Are Going To Be Strangers* (1972).

The main protagonists of *Leaving Cheyenne* never leave the country (as Lonnie did). Although Johnny does some roaming in his youth, he eventually returns to his old home county, where, like Gid and Molly, he spends the rest of his life. Molly has no desire to leave her father's ranch; she lives in the same house all her life and never leaves Archer County. Gid is even more bound to what McMurtry describes in the epigram to Gid's section as "his heart's pastureland." The one time he leaves home to go cowboying with Johnny in the panhandle, he is miserable:

I didn't mind the country, or even the cold weather. I just minded feeling like I wasn't where I belonged. Home was where I belonged. . . . I couldn't get over thinking about Dad and Molly and the country and the ranch, the things I knew. The things that were mine. It wasn't that I liked being in Archer County so much—sometimes I hated it. But I was just tied up with it; whatever happened there was happening to me, even if I wasn't there to see it. The country might not be very nice and the people might be onery; but it was my country and my people, and no other country was; no other people, either. You do better staying with what's your own, even if it's hard. [P. 106]

Significantly, Gid's section of the narrative is entitled "The Blood's Country."

The initiatory shocks that thrust Gid into his lonely manhood are the suicide of his father and the apparent defection of Molly who, although she loves Gid more than any other man, marries Eddie. Molly remains a formative force in Gid's life even after her marriage to Eddie (and Gid's ill-fated marriage to Mabel). Gid and Molly continue to be lovers for years, and Molly, whose life has been dedicated to unselfish giving, attempts to release Gid from the puritanical inhibitions that prevent him from being "whole hog in love." Molly has sensed Gid's incapacity to love uninhibitedly since the time they were adolescent. Gid bungles his first attempt to make love to Molly—immediately after he has proposed to her and has been turned down—because of his prudence.

"I'm crazy about you too, Gid," she said, hugging my neck. "You're the best to me of anybody. But I ain't going to marry, I mean it. I'll do anything you want me to but that. I'll do everything else if you want me to right now," and when I kissed her she was trembling like a leaf. But we never managed it, somehow: it was my fault. I guess I was too surprised at Molly, and I couldn't quit thinking about it. She practically took her shirt off and that was something, but I couldn't quit thinking about it, and I knew it wasn't right, so I made her quit. [p. 30]

In this same episode Gid refuses to swim in the nude with Molly. When she teases him, he becomes angry and says, "I know what's right and what ain't." She tells him, "Don't ask me to marry you any more . . . you're too sober," and he replies, "I may be too sober . . . I guess I am. But I'm not going to get stampeded into doing something crazy even if we do both want to. You got to be careful about some things." (p. 31)

Reflecting on the incident later, Gid admits, "I guess I always did think things over too much, at least where Molly was concerned." When Gid does sleep with Molly the first time, the same prudence persists: "when we got there [to her bedroom] I remembered something and left her for a minute and went and latched the screen doors. I went back and she was crying . . . 'Don't ever leave me like that again,' she said. 'I don't care if the doors are latched or not. Next time you leave me, just keep going' " (p. 51).

Molly loves Gid for more than forty years, but she can never persuade him to give of himself completely. She reflects on this in her section of the novel:

When we were both younger I could entice him to relax once in a while, but the older we got the less luck I had. Mostly, I guess, it was because Gid had so much energy he couldn't hardly stay still; but partly it was because he was ashamed of himself for being there in the first place, especially if it was in the daytime. At night he wasn't as bad, but then I never got to see much of him at night. [p. 160]

In Gid's section she explains to Gid what she means by being "whole hog in love":

"I mean just you loving me," she said. "And nothin' else. Just pure me and pure you. But you're always thinking about Johnny or Eddie or your ranch or your dad or what people will think, or what's right and what's wrong, something like that. Or else you just like to think about having me for a girl. That ain't loving nobody much. I can tell that." . . .
   "Oh, Gid," she said, and tears come in her eyes, I don't want to hurt you. I just want you to turn loose of yourself for a minute, so you can hold *me*. That's the only thing I want." (pp. 133–134)

When Gid loses Molly to Eddie, he marries Mabel because of his loneliness. Mabel is totally different from Molly, who is uninhibited in her lovemaking and uninhibited in her loving. But when Gid asks Mabel if he can make love to her, she says, "You can if you want to, Gid. . . . then we can get married and start having babies." When Gid indicates his reluctance, "she put on all the brakes." Gid soon realizes the difference between Mabel and Molly: "Molly was wild, but she was warm, and she wasn't sly. Mabel wasn't really a bit wild, but she was really cold and sly. Mabel's little brain was cold as an icicle" (p. 36). It is implicit in a conversation that Gid has with Molly after his marriage to Mabel that Mabel is frigid, as well as selfish and materialistic. Molly, on the other hand, cannot stand "not having anybody to do for":

I never was happy when I just had myself to do for, or even when I had somebody else wanting to do for me. That was nice, but that wasn't the main point about loving, at least not with me. The main point was having somebody I could let my feelings out on. And I couldn't do that very well at a distance, I needed to have somebody right around close, so I could touch them and cook for them and do little things like that. It was always men or boys, with me. I never knew a woman I cared for—not even Ma. Men need a lot of things they don't even know about themselves, and most of them they can't get nowhere but from women. It was easy to do for them, most of the time, and it made me feel so comfortable. A lot of times it wasn't easy, of course, but it still felt better to try. [P. 167]

Molly's sexuality is not indicative of an amorality on her part; rather it is symptomatic of her desire to "do for" men: "It was because a man needed it, and had it all tangled up with his pride, so that it was a sure way of helping him or hurting him, whichever you wanted to do. . . . I seen where it could really do wonderful things for a man if a woman cared to take a few pains with him" (pp. 201–202). Eddie, who married Molly "just to show up Johnny and Gid" (p. 202), was egomaniacal about sex. Animalistic and brutal, he needed her as an extension of his own ego. Johnny was hedonistic about sex ("he had more pure talent for enjoying himself than Gid and Eddie put together. . . . The right or wrong of it seldom entered Johnny's mind"). Molly says (p. 158) that one of the nicest things about Johnny was that he was like a boy ("a boy and a man in the same person. Not like Gid at all—Gid never had been a boy"). In a revealing statement about her relationship with Johnny, Molly says, "I was the only woman Johnny had ever been able to count on, and I usually tried to give him what he needed—it wouldn't have been very loving of me not to" (p. 159).

Molly always preferred Gid to the rest, yet her relationship with him was the most complicated because of his guilt-ridden attitude toward sex: "He just couldn't believe sex was right. I don't guess he left my bedroom five times in his life that he wasn't ashamed of himself—in spite of all I done" (p. 202).

Although Gid desperately loved Molly, he could seldom love her uninhibitedly. As Molly says: "The only way with Gid was to keep him from having to face what was on his mind until he was already in the bed. When I could manage that, he loved it. He loved it as much as Eddie or more; but it was just very seldom that he could let himself go" (p. 214). Even Johnny senses Gid's problem and tells him, "You're just ashamed of something that ain't shameful." And Molly isn't ashamed of what she does, even when her son Jimmy accuses her of fornication and adultery. Fornication and adultery are just mere words to Molly, "even if they do come out of the Bible. . . . The words didn't describe what I had lived with Gid, or with Johnny, at all; they didn't describe what we had felt" (p. 196).

Jimmy, like his father Gid, is puritanical in his attitude toward sex. When Jimmy is killed in the war, Gid decides to end his relationship with Molly. Molly asks him why he is ashamed of their love and says, "I always thought really caring about a person made a difference in what was right and wrong" (p. 216), but Gid persists in his guilt-ridden determination. In desperation, Molly fights to keep them together. "Gid, I'm just me," she says. "I ain't the law, and I ain't the church. All I say is, if it's wrong, then let's go ahead and have the guts to be wrong. We can't but go to hell for it, and that would be better than doing without you" (p. 216). Gid is adamant, however; it is over ten years before he ever touches Molly, and then it is only a pat on the shoulder. It is characteristic of Molly that she helps Gid keep his resolution, for "it wouldn't have been loving him much to have tricked him into doing something he had suffered so much to quit doing" (p. 219).

Kenneth Davis, in his examination of the theme of initiation in *Leaving Cheyenne*, contends that Gid, in accepting the adult responsibility of running his father's ranch, has passed through a decisive initiation into full maturity and is therefore "saved from the alienation which engulfed Lonnie Bannon."[2] The fact is, however, that Gid is far from mature at this time. Less than two weeks after his father's suicide, Gid, driven by loneliness, does "an awful ignorant thing": he marries Mabel Peters (p. 129). He immediately perceives that he has acted like a "blind idiot," for not only is Mabel cold and unloving, but he is still desperately in love with Molly. Indeed, while Molly is Gid's junior by some four years, she is nonetheless maturer emotionally. She remains Gid's only counselor after the death of his father and tries unsuccessfully to advise him on life and love. Ironically, despite her complex rationale for doing so, Molly herself marries the wrong man. The result is that her husband Eddie grows to hate her, and Gid's life is irremediably saddened.

McMurtry has said that the emotions at work in *Leaving Cheyenne* probably reflect his own marriage rather than his adolescence, and are quite complex, while the emotions underlying his next book, *The Last Picture Show*, are distaste, bitterness, and resentment against the small town.[3] McMurtry has drawn upon his own adolescent emotional experience in both *Horseman* and *The Last Picture Show*. In *Horseman*, however, he focuses upon the turmoil of young Lon Bannon and tells the story from his point of view. This affords a memorable portrait of an adolescent who comes of age on a west Texas ranch, as well as of the two adults who do so much to shape him for manhood.

The Last Picture Show, employing the third person omniscient point of view, records the emotional experience of several adolescents (Sonny, Duane, Jacy, and Joe Bob) and indicates how the town (as opposed to the country) complicates their coming of age. The approach in this novel is sociopsychological, and the cataloging of the sexual habits of the town's inhabitants disturbed early reviewers of the book. Thalia is a west Texas *Wasteland:* its inhabitants make love but seem incapable of loving; their lovemaking is merely an escape from boredom or loneliness (or, in the case of Jacy and Abilene, a narcissistic extension of ego).

The main action of the novel is concerned with the emergence into manhood of a high school senior, Sonny Crawford. His sophistication (or loss of innocence), as well as that of his peer group, is accomplished through sex. It is through the medium of sex that the inhabitants of Thalia seek (and find) their identity.

On the surface, McMurtry's treatment of small-town sexuality may seem quite sensational; actually, it is accurate. In the cloying confines of Thalia, the only outlet for frustrations, loneliness, boredom, even hatred—for both adolescents and adults—is sex. And sex, in all its versions (and perversions) is cataloged in this novel: petting, masturbation, homosexuality, bestiality, voyeurism, exhibitionism. Some of McMurtry's sexual scenes are highly symbolic, all are important thematically, and none should be taken as sensationalism.

The earliest treatment of sex in *The Last Picture Show* is the description of the adolescent sex play of Sonny and his "steady" girl, Charlene Duggs (pp. 21—23). Charlene allows Sonny a little "above the waist passion," but nothing else. Their lovemaking has become a dispassionate ritual, which, at best, is frustrating; ultimately, and inevitably, it becomes boring. This night Sonny idly holds one of Charlene's breasts in his hand. Charlene notices his apathy and asks him about it. "Sonny was disconcerted. He was not sure what was wrong. It did not occur to him that he was bored." When Sonny attempts something more exciting, Charlene is enraged. "Well, you needn't get so mad," says Sonny. "After so long a time I get tired of doing the same thing, and you do too. You wasn't no livelier than me." The night ends with their "breaking up," symbolized by Charlene's returning Sonny's football jacket to him and Sonny's returning Charlene's photographs to her. Sonny had never really loved Charlene. He was attracted instead to Jacy Farrow, the town's richest girl, and Genevieve, the kind-hearted waitress in the all-night café. But Jacy was going with Sonny's best friend, Duane, and Genevieve was married.

Duane is also having trouble with his girlfriend, Jacy. Jacy, a spoiled and egotistical rich girl, has no intention of ever marrying Duane, who roughnecks on the night shift with a drilling crew. Jacy equates sex with popularity and performs most passionately when before an audience. Jacy and Duane are the "star couple" in the necking parties during the bus ride home from the basketball games. Jacy and Duane always sat in the back seat of the bus, but Duane disliked the seat because there was a small overhead light above it that the bus driver refused to turn off ("he wasn't about to trust any kids in a totally dark bus"). Jacy, however, liked the light: "Courting with Duane when all the kids on the school bus could watch gave Jacy a real thrill, and made her feel a little like a movie star: she could bring beauty and passion into the poor kids' lives" (p. 75). There is always a touch of the histrionic (even exhibitionism) in Jacy's lovemaking: "Jacy would kiss and play around any time, but she seldom got excited past the point of control unless she was on the school bus, where people were watching. Being in the public eye seemed to heighten the quality of every touch" (p. 76). Indeed, Jacy's theatrical passion enhances her reputation at Thalia's high school.

The closing of the movie theater, which had exerted such an influence on the town's adolescents, marks the end of innocence (symbolized by Billy's death) and the emergence into adulthood of the town's youth (the last picture show was, significantly, *The Kid from Texas*). Billy, the idiot boy who swept out the pool hall and the movie house owned by Sam the Lion, symbolizes innocence. He is often the brunt of cruel pranks played by the boys, but he always remains trusting and loving. He cannot accept the fact that the movie is closed forever; "for seven years he had gone to the show every single night." One night Billy manages to slip into the balcony of the closed theater. The screen is disappointingly dead, but Billy sits in the dark for hours, patiently waiting for the show to begin, until Sonny finds him and leads him home. The most moving scene in the book is the one in which Sonny lays the dead Billy on the sidewalk in front of the closed theater. As a result of a fight over Jacy, Sonny has lost the sight of one eye, and when Billy is killed, he has both his eyes covered with Sonny's eye patches. McMurtry said that the blindness motif that runs throughout the book symbolizes the "sightlessness of life in a small town."[4] The picture show is what the inhabitants of Thalia see beyond the town; when the show closes, what is beyond the town also closes for them.

The intricacies of the tangled web of small-town sexuality are indicated in the fact that Abilene, the erstwhile lover of Lois, later seduces Lois's daughter Jacy in the poolroom. Lois, on the other hand, sleeps with Sonny on the night of his marriage to her daughter Jacy, and the wry comment about "small town life" that she makes to Sonny in the motel room (p. 255) is the best summary of the situation, for small town life is what McMurtry's third novel is about, specifically, small-town sex life.

The Last Picture Show is by no means a "Western" novel; McMurtry's Thalia could have been located in Sherwood Anderson's Ohio or William Faulkner's Mississippi. One review of the novel called it a "retreat into the literature of nostalgia," "a kind of Huckleberry Finn after the fall."[5] This interpretation is not quite accurate; McMurtry is certainly anything but nostalgic in this book. Commenting on the dedication of the novel (*"The Last Picture Show* is lovingly dedicated to my home town"), McMurtry said that it was deliberately ambiguous but that, of course, it was ironic.[6] Like Twain, McMurtry employs a native idiom, and he is also successful in presenting a realistic portrait of youth. The main difference is that Twain's Huck Finn is prepubescent and untroubled by the anxieties of adolescent sexuality. Also, Huck could escape the town and spend idyllic months on a raft with Jim; McMurtry's Sonny is landlocked in the Texas plains town of Thalia. A better comparison might be made between Sonny Crawford and Salinger's Holden Caulfield; both are postpubescent and are thus caught in the troubled period between childhood and maturity. But Salinger's adolescents are atypical, neurotic individuals who are inevitably isolated from their peer group; certainly Holden's attitude toward sex cannot be considered normal.

McMurtry's portrayal of male adolescence is realistic and frank. If the book seems obsessed with sex, it is only because the adolescent male is typically preoccupied with the subject himself. Sonny is often embarrassed by his own tumescence: "like most of his friends he went through life half-convinced that the adults of Thalia would somehow detect even his most secret erections and put them down in the book against him" (p. 34).

Masturbation is a common practice among the boys, but their attitudes toward it vary according to their level of emotional maturity. The Melly brothers often spend their lunch hour masturbating in the boys' restroom: "Freshman and sophomores got a kick out of watching them go at it, but it was really beneath the attention of seniors like Sonny and Duane" (p. 39). To Sonny, masturbation was simply a way to relieve tension when his sexual fantasies kept him awake: ("an old game, monotonous, but a good way to get to sleep when all else failed"). Both the fantasies and the remedy for them cease when Sonny begins his affair with the coach's wife, Ruth Popper.

Sonny and Duane visit brothels twice in the novel: during the wild excursion to Mexico and on their last trip together in Fort Worth. In both instances the experience is unrewarding; the exhausted Sonny falls asleep before climax in Mexico, and in Fort Worth the girls at the New Deal Hotel are "so efficient that afterward it seemed to Sonny that he and the girl had barely touched" (p. 269). (These unsatisfactory relations with prostitutes should be compared with that of young Gid and Johnny in *Leaving Cheyene*, which are similarly unsatisfying.)

In *Horseman, Pass By*, Lonnie had sought, unsuccessfully, to realize his sexual nature with Halmea, the adult Negro on his grand-father's ranch; he does not come into contact with any adolescent girls during the course of the novel. Although the first chapter of *The Last Picture Show* details a date Sonny has with his teenage steady, it is not until he begins his relationship with Ruth Popper—a woman forty years old—that sex begins to have any deep sig-nificance to him. After he has kissed an adult female (but not as yet had sexual relations with her), Sonny loses all inclination to partici-pate in the group copulation with a young heifer. When the heifer finally escapes the drunken high school youths and they decide to "breed" the idiot Billy with a local prostitute, Sonny is the only one in the ribald band to object. His objections are unheeded, however, and the boys go through with their prank, but Sonny refuses to share in their voyeuristic pleasure (pp. 108–110).

The incident marks the turning point in Sonny's maturity; when he becomes Ruth Popper's lover, he turns his back upon the sexual highjinks and escapades of the adolescent. Although he leaves Ruth briefly for Jacy Farrow, he returns to her at the end of the novel. She takes him back, knowing that ultimately she will lose him again, that "something would take him from her and the process of drying up would have to be endured again" (p. 280). But she can see that "after all, he was only a boy." Sonny's youth and vulnerability are what appeal to Genevieve and to Lois Farrow, and it is primarily through the compassion of these women that Sonny is shaped for manhood. Typically, McMurtry's male protagonists discover, or come close to discovering, the meaning of life through women who are much older than themselves; in many ways even Molly is a woman when Gid and Johnny are still boys. In the final scene of *The Last Picture Show*, Ruth Popper almost tells Sonny the secret of life:

. . . she took Sonny's young hand and pressed it to her throat, to her wet face. She was on the verge of speaking to him, of saying something fine. It seemed to her that on the tip of her tongue was something it had taken her forty years to learn, something wise or brave or beautiful that she could finally say. It would be just what Sonny needed to know about life, and she would have said it if her own relief had not been so strong. [p. 280]

The themes of loneliness and lost love recur in McMurtry's novels, but the most important theme in the first three novels is the male protagonists' achievement of manhood (with its accompanying loss of innocence). These males are accompanied in their rites of passage by women who are older or, as in the case of Molly, more sophisticated in their emotional maturity.

II   *Loneliness*

In his first three novels, McMurtry has written about life in the country and in the dead or dying little towns of west Texas. In doing so, he has chronicled what becomes a major theme in his early fiction: the initiation into manhood and its inevitable corollaries—loneliness and loss of innocence.

McMurtry's first novel, *Horseman, Pass By*, exhibits the initiation theme that he develops in his later novels. A general feeling of loneliness permeates this first book. In the prologue, Lonnie speaks of how the saddest and loneliest time of day, twilight, was passed on the Bannon ranch. The whole family would gather on the front porch, and in the fading light they would watch the cars rushing across the plains on the highway a mile away. The growl of the big diesel trucks reached them through the thick prairie dusk, and during the shipping season the freights chugged by with carloads of calves. The bawling of the calves "was a lonesome sound at twilight," and it often made the grandfather think of "other times he had heard it, and of the men he had heard it with" (p. 4). It was then that he told stories about cowboys like his dead foreman, Jericho Green. But the saddest sound of all was the whistle of the nightly

Zephyr, which always made the old man restless and sent him off to bed. After his grandfather was in bed, Lonnie would climb up and sit atop the windmill, staring at the lights of a little town twelve miles across the plain.

Scraps of hillbilly songs often underscore the loneliness of the characters. In one scene, Lonnie moodily flips a stick into a big water tank and watches it bob in the water. He recalls, "It made me think of an old hillbilly song by Moon Mulligan, called 'I'll Sail My Ship Alone.' With all the dreams I own. Sail it out across the ocean blue." Similarly, a scrap of song underscores the loneliness of the cowboy, Jesse, who has always been a womanless wanderer. "Fraulein, fraulein, look down from your window and be mine," sings Jesse, then slumps back in his seat with a sigh. "Ain't no fraulein ever looked down on me," he tells Lonnie; "not unless it was to ask for money. Some fellers just belong in whorehouses, I don't know why." Even the fiercely independent Hud is sometimes lonely. When Hud asks Jesse and Lonnie if they want to go into town with him, Lonnie is

. . . so surprised I didn't say anything, but Jesse grinned and shook his head. "No thanks for me," he said. "I'm gonna stay here and scare up a checker game."

"I guess that is about your speed," Hud said. He got into his convertible and left, with us standing there watching him.

"That's the first time in my life he ever asked me to go anywhere," I said. "I wonder why he did it."

Jesse took a package of cigarettes out of his pocket. "Lonesome, I imagine," he said. "Just tryin' to scare up a little company."

"Him lonesome?" I said. "Why he can get more women company than anybody around here."

"That ain't necessarily much," Jesse said. "It ain't necessarily company, neither. Women just like to be around something dangerous part of the time. Scott ain't so mean but what he could get lonesome once in a while." [p. 82]

Lonnie's loneliness, however, differs from that of the adults in the book. His grandfather's loneliness occurs primarily in the evening, when the sights and sounds of twilight recall days spent on the prairie in his youth; it is the product of an old man's nostalgia for the old days. Halmea seems to have reconciled herself to a lonely life; she often chuckles and dances "her lonesome happy dance" (p. 26). Jesse, on the other hand, broods, and "a big loneliness hangs over him" (p. 34). His loneliness results from his own self-pitying conviction that he can never be anything but a drifter. In an early scene in the book, Jesse and Halmea discuss marriage. He tells Halmea, "A poor boy like me's got to be lucky to get along, just like it is, and if he's got a family he needs to be two or three times as lucky. So far I ain't even been lucky enough for myself" (p. 17). But Halmea counters, "Sheew, don't tell me. A man by himself just like de fishline without de hook. He ain't gonna snag on nothin', dat away." And, of course, an occasional loneliness might be expected even in such a loner as Hud. Lonnie's loneliness, however, is that strange mixture of restlessness, longing, and frustration so typical of the male adolescent. The same train that depresses his grandfather fills Lonnie with wanderlust: "I could see the hundred lighted windows of the passenger cars, and I wondered where in the world the people behind them were going night after night. To me it was exciting to think about a train. But the Zephyr blowing by seemed to make Grandad tireder; seemed to make him sad" (p. 4).

The Bannon ranch is isolated, and the town of Thalia, twelve miles away, offers little excitement. When Jesse asks Lonnie, "What do kids do for fun around here?", a brief exchange between Lonnie and Lonzo ensues. " 'Whatever there is,' " I said. 'What the hell is there?' Lonzo said. 'About a dime's worth is all I can see.' " Lonnie admits to the reader: "Actually we didn't do an awful lot. There was the pool hall, the snooker and eight-ball tables. But most of the time we just rode around and talked, or hunted up girls to court. Once in a while we drove to the county line and bought some beer" (p. 36).

At night there is nothing open in Thalia but a single movie house and an all-night trucker's café. Both Jesse and Lonzo have seen considerably more of the world than Lonnie, who has spent only three nights in Fort Worth, and Jesse's reminiscences make Lonnie even more eager to see the world: "What little Jesse had said about his running around just made me a little more restless than I usually was, and I was usually crazy with it. I wished I had something wild and exciting to do. But I didn't have an old wired-up Chevy, and it was too late to go anywhere in the pickup, and if I had taken it and gone there would just have been Thalia to go to, just an empty courthouse square to drive around" (p. 20). Lonnie's restless loneliness, his frustrated sense of unfulfillment, is characteristic of the adolescent's awakening sexuality.

The loneliness that permeates *Leaving Cheyenne* is a different type. Gideon Fry, for instance, has certainly been initiated sexually;

he has caught a venereal disease and has had to go to Kansas for a cure before his narrative begins. Gid's loneliness is symptomatic of his wasted life that results from his love for a woman. This loneliness accompanies him on the train trip to the Texas panhandle with his best friend Johnny and on the trip back, alone; it gnaws at him in crowds, and it is not lessened when he marries Mabel Peters, not even during the first month of marriage. "I never was bluer than I was that first month," says Gid. "If a feller has to be lonesome, he's better off being lonesome alone" (p. 130). And Molly, bereft of father, husband, sons, and, ultimately, Gid, spends most of her adult life in lonely isolation on her father's old homestead. There is no remission of the loneliness in *Leaving Cheyenne;* it lasts the lifetime of the three central characters in the novel.

The same might be said of the loneliness that afflicts the life of Ruth Popper, the coach's wife in *The Last Picture Show.* Though she gains a brief requital in her desperate affair with her young lover, Sonny Crawford, Ruth senses that "it would only be a year or two or three before it would all repeat itself" (p. 279), and that she would again be alone. Indeed, the loneliness that is such a dominant motif in McMurtry's first two novels is omnipresent in *The Last Picture Show,* which begins, "Sometimes Sonny felt like he was the only human creature in the town." Sonny's loneliness is echoed in the lives of the adults: Ruth Popper, Genevieve Morgan, Sam the Lion, and Lois Farrow. The loneliness of the adults is underscored by their realization that they are growing old. "Goddammit! Goddammit!" exclaims Sam the Lion. "I don't want to be old. It don't fit me!" (p. 153), and after reminiscing about his old love, he says, "Being crazy about a woman like her's always the right thing to do. Being a decrepit old bag of bones is what's ridiculous" (p. 154). Sam is constantly being reminded of his lost youth by the boys. So is Genevieve, who is saddened when Sonny and Duane depart for their trip to Mexico. "The boys had made her remember what it was to be young. . . . Romance might not last, but it was something while it did. . . . She went back into the empty café, wishing for a few minutes that she was young again and free and could go rattling off across Texas toward the Rio Grande" (pp. 165–66). Ruth Popper "hated being old and despised Jacy Farrow for being young" (p. 229). The loneliness of her married life is briefly relieved by her affair with Sonny, but when she loses him to Jacy, she despairs. "She tried to remember herself when she was young, tried to recall one time in her life when she had been as attractive as Jacy, but she couldn't think of one. It seemed to her she had always been old" (p. 230). Even the hardened, cynical Lois is moved when she notices Jacy's youth and Sonny's young vulnerability.

Sonny himself experiences the feeling of growing old, which accentuates his own feeling of isolation and loneliness. When the football boys troop into the café after their workout, Sonny feels "left out" and depressed: "He had always been on the football team and had done the same things they were doing after workouts, but suddenly he wasn't on the team and the boys didn't even notice him, he might have been out of high school ten years" (p. 257). Later, when Sonny attends the high school football game, he notices that the grass on the field looks "greener and softer than it ever had when he played," and when the assistant coach asks him to run the first-down chain, Sonny momentarily identifies with the crowd: "When the band played the Thalia song it was a little thrilling: it touched something in Sonny and made him feel as though he was part of it again, the high school, football, the really important part of life in the town" (p. 259). Soon, however, Sonny realizes that he is not a part of it at all. He keeps wishing that he were on the field, running plays, or even on the bench with the freshmen and sophomores, who were at least "suited out." But Sonny was only on the sidelines, a mere spectator: "Running the chain, measuring first downs, that was nothing: he might have been invisible to everyone but the referees. He was an ex-student—nothing. A feeling came over him sort of like the feelings he used to get in the mornings, only the new feeling was worse. Then he had felt like he was the only one in town, but standing on the sidelines, holding the chain, he felt like he wasn't even *in* town—he felt like he wasn't anywhere" (p. 260). Sonny also feels lonely in the riotous celebration that ensues after Thalia wins the game. "People he had known all his life were all around him, but they simply didn't see him. He was out of school" (p. 261).

The loneliness the characters in the book feel combines with the boredom of the small town to cause them to seek an escape in sex. This is certainly the case with Lois Farrow, whose cynicism and ennui are apparent in almost every conversation she has with her daughter. "Oh, don't be so mealy-mouthed," she tells Jacy, "I just thought if you slept with Duane a few times you'd find out there really isn't anything magic about him, and have yourself some fun to boot" (p. 48). In the same conversation, she says: "The only really

important thing I came in to tell you was that life is very monotonous. Things happen the same way over and over again. I think it's
more monotonous in this part of the country than it is in other
places, but I don't really know that—it may be monotonous
everywhere. I'm sick of it, myself. Everything gets old if you do it
often enough" (p. 49). With this remark Lois leaves her daughter.
"To kill the morning she had gone to Wichita Falls and spent $150
to kill the afternoon she had three drinks and several rubbers of
bridge at the country club. It seemed unjust that after all that work
she should still have the problem of how to kill the night." After
considering a moment she pours herself a drink and telephones the
pool hall to make an overture to the town's rake, Abilene. When her
effort fails, she pours herself another drink and settles down to
watch the late movie on television (pp. 49–50).

Adulthood accentuates the loneliness of adolescence; Sonny's own
painful emergence into adulthood is predicted in the conversation
he has with Sam the Lion: " 'Is growin' up always miserable?' Sonny
said. 'Nobody seems to enjoy it much.' 'Oh, it ain't necessarily
miserable,' Sam replied. 'About eighty percent of the time, I
guess' " (p. 154).

The final chapter of *The Last Picture Show* operates as a framing
device with the first; the mood of the opening line of the novel—
"Sometimes Sonny felt like he was the only human creature in
town"—is repeated in the final chapter when Sonny "had the feeling
again, the feeling that he was the only person in town" (p. 277). He
drives his pickup truck past the city limits of Thalia where the "gray
pastures and the distant brown ridges looked too empty." He cannot
break free from the confines of the town or the loneliness within
him: "As empty as he felt and as empty as the country looked it was
too risky going out into it—he might be blown around for days like a
broomweed in the wind" (p. 277), and he is drawn back into the
town and the arms of his aging paramour, Ruth Popper.

To flee the town would have been futile. As the protagonists of
McMurtry's urban novels attest, neither the open highways nor the
streets of Houston or Los Angeles offer respite from the loneliness
that grips the wanderers of *All My Friends Are Going To Be Strangers* and *Moving On*. Driving his Chevy through the soft warm night,
Danny realizes, "There just wasn't any prospect of anybody, up any
of the roads I might drive. I sat in the car on the street of McAllen,
watching the other cars go by. I didn't know why I was so alone. I

had never really felt quite so alone" (*All My Friends*, p. 264). Similarly, Eleanor Guthrie, the rich heiress in *Moving On*, can find no
cure for her restless loneliness: "Eleanor lay on her bed reading
about Peru. . . . She had traveled a good deal in Central and South
America, but for some reason had never been to Peru. . . . In the
spring and in the fall she became restless, unable to be still, unin-
terested in the ranch and the ranch work and money and Texas, and
she left. Lima had a lovely name" (p. 190). Patsy Carpenter has the
same gnawing loneliness, though she should have felt fulfilled:
"Patsy had never thought of herself as a lonely person and had never
believed that loneliness would be a problem—not for her. . . . She
had read a lot about loneliness and knew it was one of the great
problems of modern life, but it had never been very real to her"
(p. 393). Yet despite her family, her friend Emma, her husband,
her child, and her lover, Patsy is lonely and restless throughout
the novel. Indeed, a sense of futility and loneliness seems to be
symptomatic of the general malaise that afflicts the world of McMurtry, a world characterized always by the loss of something—youth,
innocence, happiness, loved ones.

III *Ephemerality*

The most pervasive theme in McMurtry's work is a sense of loss,
of things passing, and the mood of this theme is reflected in the
titles McMurtry has chosen for his books. The titles always contain a
note of ephemerality, and even those of early drafts of the published
novels, as well as those of unpublished works and abandoned projects, share this characteristic (for example, *Our Revels Now Are
Ended*,[7] *Lovebreaking*,[8] *Take My Saddle From the Wall*,[9] *Memories
of the Old Tribe*, [10] *Lonely Singer, Lonely Song*[11]). In the introduction to *In a Narrow Grave* (p. xv), McMurtry writes that he was
originally going to entitle the book *The Cowboy in the Suburbs* but
chose *In a Narrow Grave* instead because he "wanted a tone that
was elegiac rather than sociological." He makes the same point in
"The Questions a Writer Gets Asked," adding that at one time he
had also considered entitling the collection of essays *Take My Saddle from the Wall*, "a title drawn, like 'Leaving Cheyenne,' from a
cowboy song, a song which has a natural congruity to the subject I
am treating. In writing about the passing of the cowboy, what better
title-source than a cowboy song, a song, moreover, explicitly about
the death of a cowboy."[12] McMurtry says that the title *Take My*

Saddle from the Wall is "elegiac in the sense that *Horseman, Pass By* and *Leaving Cheyenne* are elegiac," and as a consequence he felt freer than he would have if he had used *The Cowboy in the Suburbs:* he could "attempt an elegy, rather than a sociological essay" and thus evoke the way of life that is ending, rather than anatomizing it."[13]

Commenting on the elegiac quality of the titles of his fictional works, McMurtry has said, "All of my titles are essentially elegiac, they are always suggestive of something passing, or a way of life coming to an end:"

All My Friends Are Going To Be Strangers clearly carries an ambiguous significance which I like very much. I never liked the title *Moving On.* I didn't choose it; it was a last minute choice. The publishers moved the publication date up six months—they had meant to publish in the spring of 1970, and this was only three days before they had to go to the printers with their catalog copy. The book had more or less floundered around for three years without a title. I thought I had another six months to get a title and suddenly I had to get a title immediately and I don't respond well that way. A title has to come to me naturally and usually it comes to me before I begin the book. This was the one case when it hadn't and I think this was because the book outgrew its original conception—it became something different from the book I set out to write. This [the title] was a choice from many mediocre choices; it seemed as good as any because the book does have a quality of "moving on" about it; so I settled on it but I was never happy with it. In all my titles there is a sense of something passing. I think, qualitatively speaking, *All My Friends* is the first different title of the six titles.[14]

Actually, *Moving On* had borne other titles, in its various textual versions, before its publication in 1970. An early typescript of the novel, completed in the late summer or early fall of 1964, was entitled *The Water and the Blood,* a title suggested by the old hymn, "Rock of Ages."[15] Still other drafts of the novel were entitled *The Country of the Horns,* and *Sometimes the Matador.*[16]

The writing of the novel and the determination of its proper title proved to be a long and difficult problem for McMurtry; indeed, the former seems to be dependent upon the latter in his creative process. McMurtry has said, "I have spoken at some length about titles because I believe they go a long way toward determining books." In supporting this statement, he alludes to an unnamed novel, but obviously he is referring to what was published as *Moving On:* "Between *Leaving Cheyenne* and *The Last Picture Show* lies a long unpublished novel which I have written four times, at about 200,000 words a time, without resolving it to my satisfaction. I have never found a title for it, never known what to call it, and I hope, still, that someday I will find a title for it and from that perhaps find the book."[17]

McMurtry draws his titles from varied sources: Shakespeare (*Our Revels Now Are Ended*), Yeats (*Horseman, Pass By*), and music (*The Water and the Blood, Leaving Cheyenne*). He has commented on the sources of his titles and his motivation for the choices:

Picking titles is one of the few pure pleasures writing offers—or so I have always found—and I get mine from a diversity of places: poetry, conversations, etc. Lately I have been finding them in the lyrics of hillbilly songs, or old Protestant hymns. The music, in most cases, may be bad, but it has a very close relation to the lives of the people who sing it. Some people live out their lives within the emotional terms of such music, and the lyrics have a natural congruity to the subjects I treat. . . . Since most of my books deal with loss—with the passing of a way of life, or at least, the passing of a time of life, I try to choose titles that have an elegiac quality, that suggest change and loss: *Horseman, Pass By* and *Leaving Cheyenne*."[18]

The title *Horseman, Pass By* is from William Butler Yeats's poem, "Under Ben Bulben," which ends with the inscription on a tombstone,

> Cast a cold eye
> On life, on death
> Horseman, pass by!

McMurtry uses Yeats's epitaph to set the tone of *Horseman, Pass By*, and the final line of the last chapter ends with Lonnie standing in the churchyard "thinking of the horseman that had passed," his grandfather, Homer Bannon (p. 174).

The title *Leaving Cheyenne*, although taken from the cowboy ballad, refers not to the city in Wyoming but to "the land of youth, the blood's country."[19] The original title of the book was *Memories of the Old Tribe*.[20] Both the original and the final have the "sense of something passing" that McMurtry has noted in his comments on the titles of his books.[21] McMurtry might have been prompted to use *Leaving Cheyenne* for the novel title rather than the nonfiction book by a letter from John Leggett, his editor at Harper's. On June 13, 1962, Leggett advised McMurtry: "I should think we'd want one fabulous color shot for the jacket of *Rodeo* or *Leaving Cheyanne* [*sic*] (let's save *Leaving Cheyanne* [*sic*] for the novel. Why not call Rodeo *Rodeo?*)."[22]

The Last Picture Show was originally intended as the title for a collection of short stories, which was never completed but which was similar in tone to the novel that ultimately bore the title. The collection was intended "to dramatize the effects of the gradual seepage of people out of the small town."[23]

IV Marriage

McMurtry's six novels reveal a consistently cynical attitude about marriage, for none of the marriages of his characters are successful. The only exceptions, by implication, are the first marriage of Homer Bannon in *Horseman, Pass By* and the marriage of Roger Wagonner in *Moving On*, but both of these have ended years before the novels begin and are only memories in the minds of the old men. Indeed, Homer Bannon's second marriage (to Hud's mother) is not fortuitous. As Hud tells him, "You thought you was goin' to die, and you got Ma to nurse you, an' she thought the same thing, an' you ended up marryin' her. Then you got well an' found out she wasn't such a bargain." (p. 78). The incompatibility of Homer and his wife is illustrated by the fact that the old couple disagree so over their choice of radio programs that each has a radio blaring away competitively in the living room: "Grandma and Grandad were there, each one sitting by a separate radio. They disagreed over the programs so much that they couldn't get along with just one. . . . the two programs blaring so loud against each other made me want to grit my teeth. It gave me the terrible feeling that things were all out of kilter, all jumbled up" (pp. 84–85).

All of the marriages in McMurtry's fiction are "out of kilter." In *Leaving Cheyenne*, Gid's father, speaking from personal experience, warns Gid about the perils of marriage. "A woman is a wonderful thing," he says, "but a man oughtn't to marry one unless he just absolutely has to have some kids. There's no other excuse" (p. 77). Gid's sweetheart, Molly, is also against marriage and repeatedly rejects Gid's attempts to legitimize their passion. "I don't want to marry you or nobody else," she tells him. "I ain't gonna marry till I have to because of having a baby, and I mean that too. And I wish I didn't even have to then" (p. 29). When Gid marries Mabel out of loneliness and frustration, he discovers immediately that he had "done an awful ignorant thing," for "if a feller has to be lonesome, he's better off being lonesome alone" (pp. 129–130). Gid's married life with Mabel is a loveless, frustrating relationship.

The attention paid to marriage in McMurtry's fiction intensifies as the novels move from the ranch setting of *Horseman, Pass By* and *Leaving Cheyenne* to the small-town setting of Thalia in *The Last Picture Show*. In this novel, McMurtry's attitude toward marriage becomes even more pessimistic; as Ruth Popper tells her husband, Herman, "Marriage is a bad joke, isn't it" (p. 194).

Lois Farrow cynically counsels her daughter, Jacy, about love and marriage. Lois's husband Gene had grown rich in the oil business, but his millions had not brought happiness to their marriage. As Lois tells Jacy: "I scared your Daddy into getting rich. He's so scared of me that for twenty years he's done nothing but run around trying to find things to please me. He's never found the right things but he made a million dollars looking" (p. 47). McMurtry had written of the loveless marriage of the new rich in his essay, "Eros in Archer County": "when they began to come into the money it was natural that they should over-rate it and expect the wrong things of it. They had imagined it would make them happier with one another, and they resented one another all the more when it didn't. Men made money and women spent it. If one spent unstintingly, sexual poverty might be disguised" (p. 70). Lois Farrow's marriage is precisely the type McMurtry describes in his essay. Lois spends money recklessly, drinks heavily, and has affairs, but is unable to escape from the boredom of her existence.

Like the Farrows in *The Last Picture Show*, the oil-rich Texans in *Moving On* are also miserable in their dull, loveless marriages. The brief description of Patsy Carpenter's parents, Garland and Jeanette White, indicates that money has brought them not happiness but boredom and, in Garland's case, a drinking habit (pp. 273–274). Similarly, the heiress Eleanor Guthrie had married a millionaire sixteen years her senior who proved to be a homosexual. They lived together for eight years "in honorable wretchedness" until he committed suicide in the restroom of a Dallas hotel (p. 135).

Not only the rich have unhappy marriages in *Moving On;* indeed, the book is essentially about the dissolution of the marriage of the main character, Patsy Carpenter. The first marriage of the rodeo clown, Pete Tatum, was unhappy. His first wife, Marie, was unfaithful to him and eventually left him, and when his second wife, Boots, becomes pregnant he has to leave the rodeo life he loves and settle down to a banal existence selling used cars for his father-in-law (pp. 653–654). The college professor and his wife, Bill and Lee Duffin, have a strained relationship, held together only by their allowing each other intermittent infidelities. The marriage of Patsy's Aunt Dixie had not lasted, Patsy's own marriage to Jim terminates in separation, and the marriage of Emma and Flap Horton remains on shaky grounds.

All the marriages in *All My Friends Are Going To Be Strangers* are either unhappy or end in divorce. Like Patsy in *Moving On*, Danny Deck, the protagonist, has an ill-fated marriage, which ends in separation. The marriage of Danny's Uncle Laredo is the most caustic portrait of marriage that McMurtry has drawn. The old couple are so incompatible that they live on separate ranches and seldom communicate even when they eat together. "Evidently conversation was not what they had married for. Probably she was determined to outlast him and get his ranch. Probably he was determined to outlast her and get hers. The determination to outlast was the bond that joined them" (p. 196).

The almost immediate deterioration of Danny's marriage to Sally is observed by his rich and frustrated neighbor, Jenny Salomea, who is married to a homosexual. In an overt sexual overture to Danny, Jenny sums up her views on their marriages: "Your marriage is nothing, okay. . . . You married a bitch and she doesn't love you and she won't stay put. So what? I married a queer. He hates the way I smell, even. Tough luck for both of us. It happens to a million people a day. . . . Come on upstairs and help me have a little fun" (p. 42).

While in California and estranged from his wife, Danny has a brief sexual encounter with the rich novelist Renata Morris. Renata's marital status is indeterminate, but it is apparently unhappy or at least meaningless (p. 115). While in California he falls in love with Jill Peel, a strange girl who had been unhappily married before, presumably because of her sexual frigidity. The marriage of Willis and Andrea Beach, acquaintances of Danny and Sally in San Francisco, is as unstable as that of their friends in Houston, Emma and Flap Horton.

Emma writes a letter to Danny while he is in California and discusses her opinion that marriages terminate friendships. When he returns to Houston, Danny has a brief affair with Emma, and

Emma tells him what has happened to her marriage. "Flap's bored with me and goes off with his dad fishing every weekend and I resent the hell out of that. . . . He doesn't like to fish that much—he's just bored. I don't resent him being bored. I just resent him going off with his dad. His dad's just as boring as me. But that's no problem, that's just normal. Two people get married and pretty soon one person is bored" (p.241).

The marriage of Emma and Flap Horton completely disintegrates in *Terms of Endearment,* a novel in which there are also no portraits of successful marriages. It is implicit that the marriage of Emma's widowed mother, Aurora Greenway, was dull, and Aurora has no intention of ever remarrying, settling instead for a host of lovers and suitors. As she tells Emma, "Marital arrangements don't happen to interest me, that's all" (p. 388). Emma's first lover, Sam Burns, has been unhappily married for twenty-six years when their affair begins. "That means you have at least twice the excuse I have," Emma tells him. "I've only been married eleven years" (p. 363). Emma's second lover, Hugh, is a recently divorced colleague of her husband, and Melba, her best friend and confidante in the little academic community of Kearney, is also involved in a loveless marriage. "Melba's husband Dick had no interest in anything but drinking, hunting, and sports—his general disregard of Melba made Flap seem almost oppressively considerate" (p. 389). Indeed, there are no fortuitous marriages in *Terms of Endearment,* whether it be in the upper ranks of society, illustrated by Aurora and her suitors, the middle class, personified by the displaced academics and small town Midwesterners of Emma's acquaintance, or the lower spectrum of society, illustrated by the marriages of Rosie Dunlup and her daughter Elfrida.

If McMurtry's novels are examined from the standpoint of the dates of their compositions, what is revealed is an increasing interest in modern marriage. When I questioned McMurtry about the persistence of the dissolution of marriage as a motif in his fiction, he expressed surprise, saying that he was unaware of it. After I enumerated the many examples he responded, "I guess I just haven't known many happy marriages; I guess I just haven't experienced that."[24]

CHAPTER 4

Characterization

M cMURTRY'S characters generally fall into recognizable types; indeed, in the more satiric passages of *The Last Picture Show*, some of them approach stereotypes. His female characters are usually maturer or are stronger emotionally than the males (notable exceptions are the aging patriarchs, Homer Bannon, Sam the Lion, and Roger Wagonner), and they are thus more interesting than his males, whether adolescents, college students, cowboys and rodeo stars, professors, or highway patrolmen. McMurtry is weakest in portraying the ethnic types of the non-Anglo subculture of the Southwest. In a response to a hostile review of *Moving On* in the *Texas Observer*, McMurtry admits that his characterization and dialogue of the black hippie are inept.[1] McMurtry does not understand the Negro character, although his portrait of the black housekeeper, Halmea, is both credible and moving. His portraits of Mexicans or Chicanos are inevitably stereotypic and unflattering, exhibiting, perhaps, a regional bias; however, when the ethnic character is a female (as in the case of the Mexican prostitute, Juanita), the character assumes a quiet dignity, particularly when juxtaposed with the immature Anglo male (Lonnie in Halmea's case, Danny in Juanita's case).

I *Women*

The importance of McMurtry's female characters to his fiction cannot be overemphasized. Even in the more episodic of his novels, such as *Leaving Cheyenne* and *Moving On*, the females dominate the action. *Leaving Cheyenne* might well have been entitled *Molly* and, similarly, *Moving On* is essentially Patsy's book. Typically, McMurtry's female characters function significantly in the maturation process of his male protagonists. In fact, the initiation and maturation of McMurtry's male characters are the inevitable corol-

70

lary of their association with women who are older or who are more mature emotionally. Often these women act as mother surrogates for the male protagonists and play important roles in their emotional development; such is the case with Lon and Halmea in *Horseman, Pass By*, Sonny and Genevieve in *The Last Picture Show*, and, to a certain extent, Gid and Molly in *Leaving Cheyenne*. In other instances, the women, although old enough to serve as mother surrogates, function as sexual objects, as with Lois Farrow and Ruth Popper in *The Last Picture Show*, both of whom contribute to Sonny's sexual sophistication.[2]

Lon *(Horseman, Pass By)*, Gid *(Leaving Cheyenne)*, Sonny *(The Last Picture Show)*, and Danny *(All My Friends Are Going To Be Strangers)* are motherless boys. When Danny Deck reflects on his precipitate and disastrous marriage to Sally, he says, "No one had told me not to marry Sally. It was because I didn't have a family to advise me. Momma was dead and Daddy and my brothers too busy running their Pontiac agency to advise me about my life" (p. 107). In the Mexican bordello, Danny is drawn naturally to the oldest prostitute, Juanita, who is also a mother: "It was the dignity of her face that had made her stand out among the teen-age whores" (p. 268). Juanita gave him the solace he needed after his traumatic experiences with his wife, Sally, and his mistress, Jill. "A woman of some experience had passed a practical judgment. . . . Someone appreciated something about me. In my whole life I had never felt so certain that I was more or less a good man" (p. 269).

Inez Hernandez Tovar has examined the role of the female as guide and mother surrogate.[3] Tovar demonstrates that McMurtry's female character "exerts a magnetic pull over the protagonist as she teaches him about life and love. She is wiser, more mature, compassionate and giving than her pupil. She has accepted herself and tries to guide the protagonist into a self-identity and acceptance. McMurtry consistently shows her to be the support and the source of stability and comfort for his maturing adolescent."[4] Tovar confines her study to the role of women in McMurtry's first three novels. In a later examination of McMurtry's females, Jimmie Clifton Sniffen argues that "a study of the mythological, sociological, and psychological aspects of Larry McMurtry's novels reveals that the women characters emerge as increasingly important to the novels and to the changing West Texas Society."[5] Sniffen contends that the women emerge as "reluctant leaders of society" and that "their leadership is

reaffirmed and strengthened by the sociological aspects of the
novels which depict a gradual change in social order from a patriar-
chy to a matriarchy."[6] Sniffen's argument is overstated, however;
although McMurtry's women are strong earth mother figures, they
are not aggressive enough to emerge as matriarchal leaders. They
are emotionally stronger than the men and are wiser in the ways of
the world and the mysteries of life, but they ultimately remain the
eternal female rather than the feminist, and their role is primarily
supportive.

Billie Phillips takes a different psychological approach.[7] Phillips
sees McMurtry's female characters as "central characters in the
sense of being directional spirits for the men," who "contain within
themselves, as does the archetypal Eternal Feminine, the potential
for creation as well as for destruction." Phillips contends that in
varying degrees McMurtry's female characters exemplify the four
kinds of love that Rollo May recognizes in Western tradition: "One
is sex, or what we call lust, *Libido*. The second is *eros*, the drive of
love to procreate or create—the urge, as the Greeks put it, toward
higher forms of being and relationship. A third is *philia*, or friendship, brotherly love. The fourth is *agape* or *caritas* as the Latins
called it, the love which is devoted to the welfare of the other. . . .
Every human experience of authentic love is a blending, in varying
proportions, of these four."[8]

Concerning the mother-surrogate figure in his fiction, McMurtry
comments, "It is obvious that my books contain very motherly
women, in some cases, and lots of women get pregnant. I don't have
much to say about that—people can make what they want of it—
there are a lot of motherly women in the world."[9] There are, however, many examples of the motherly aspects of McMurtry's matronly (if seductive) females. For instance, Sonny Crawford is attracted to Genevieve Morgan, the waitress at the all-night café in
The Last Picture Show. "She was beginning to thicken a bit at the
waist, but she was still pretty, high-breasted and long-legged"
(p. 28), and Sonny was strongly affected by her. She was even more
attractive than the teenage beauty, Jacy Farrow: "Even Jacy didn't
affect him quite as strongly; beside Genevieve, Jacy seemed
strangely diminished, and apparently Jacy knew it" (p. 31).
Genevieve is aware that Sonny is infatuated with her, but her attitude toward him remains essentially maternal. When Sonny and
Duane return from a wild trip to Fort Worth to the all-night café,

Genevieve feeds them (the mother figures are always associated with warm kitchens and food), and "as soon as they ate a little they dozed off and slept with their heads on the counter. . . . Asleep they both had the tousled, helpless look of young children and she kept wanting to cover their shoulders or something" (p. 66).

Unlike Genevieve, Lois Farrow's motherly attitude causes her to seduce Sonny on the night of his abortive wedding to her daughter (p. 251ff.). Similarly, the childless Ruth Popper's affair with Sonny takes on a maternal aspect in her strange fantasies during their lovemaking. During the first stages of their affair, Ruth does not achieve orgasm during intercourse: "For her the beautiful time was still afterward. Sonny was still inside her when he went to sleep, and Ruth found that lovely. It was almost as if he were a child inside her, and she put her calves over his legs to keep him there. When he finally came out she slipped upward on the quilt so that his warm cheek was against one of her breasts" (p. 124). Later Ruth dreams that she gives birth to Sonny. "She dreamed she was having a baby. She had had such dreams for years, but usually they were vague and fragmentary, but this one was vivid. It was not just a baby she had; it was Sonny. He was removed from between her legs, and afterward lay at her breast" (pp. 128–29). The next time that Ruth and Sonny have intercourse, Ruth remembers the dream: "Because of the dream, pleasure took her over: with her eyes shut she could pretend she was giving birth. Sonny was inside her but in truth she was bringing him out—it was that which excited her," and for the first time in their affair, Ruth succeeds in having an orgasm, almost fainting "with the relief of delivery" (p. 129).

The mother figures are just as often associated with food as with sex. Genevieve is usually seen in the all-night restaurant where she is always ready to dispense hot coffee, hamburgers, compassion, and sympathy at any time of the night. Emma Horton is not older than Danny Deck, but her pleasing rotundity gives her a matronly look, which Danny likes, and the warmth of her kitchen is always reassuring to him. Emma constantly feeds Danny in her kitchen, and Jenny Salomea feeds him and makes love to him on the giant wood block in her kitchen. The deeply depressed Danny muses on the symbolic warmth of Emma's kitchen before wading into the river at the end of the novel: "The door to the ordinary places was the door that I had missed. The door to Emma's kitchen, or to all such places. There would never be an Emma's kitchen for me" (p. 281).

Commenting on the role women play in the maturation process of his male characters, McMurtry said that he did not "consciously" cast his women as the "initiators" of his men, yet at least one of his characters, Danny Deck, whom McMurtry considers to be the most mature and perceptive of his males, contradicts this denial. In a moment of self-analysis, Danny says: "No more feeling sorry for myself. Why should I? None of my models in life felt sorry for themselves. Not Emma, not Jenny, not Jill. Not Juanita. It was odd that all my models in life were women, but no odder than a lot of things" (p.272).

Although McMurtry argued that "it is a very common thing in literature, and in life, that young men are attracted to older women,"[10] he seems almost preoccupied with the phenomenon in his novels, as in the examples of Halmea in *Horseman, Pass By*, Genevieve Morgan, Ruth Popper, and Lois Farrow in *The Last Picture Show*, Jenny Salomea and Juanita in *All My Friends Are Going To Be Strangers*, and Eleanor Guthrie and Lee Duffin in *Moving On*. Ultimately, McMurtry admitted, "By and large, across the board, women are more mature than men, are stronger, emotionally, in some ways. It's something that I doubtlessly reflect in my fiction. Of course I am interested in all kinds of women, but I'm more interested in the strong and mature women, and always have been, really."[11] McMurtry is obviously alluding to Halmea, Genevieve, Ruth, Lois, Jenny, and Eleanor when he refers to "strong and mature women," but if Molly, in *Leaving Cheyenne*, is the same age as her lovers, she is certainly more mature emotionally, and if Patsy Carpenter in *Moving On* is at first as emotionally immature as her husband and her lover, she gradually progresses toward maturity and self-knowledge while Jim and Hank remain essentially static. Even the older women who are not particularly strong (for example, Genevieve and Eleanor) are nonetheless invariably interesting. Lee Duffin, although incompletely developed as a character, is infinitely more interesting than her philandering husband, and Dixie McCormick, a scatterbrained eccentric, is nonetheless lovable. Dixie belongs to the type more fully developed in *Terms of Endearment*, a novel which centers around the character of Emma Horton's mother who is "all that Emma isn't: she is wildly selfish, wildly irresponsible, crazy, demanding, kicky, arrogant, and yet, an extremely endearing and lovable woman. But she does not possess any of the virtues of the normal wife and mother."[12]

McMurtry's choice of words in his description of Emma's mother, "the virtues of the normal wife and mother," reveals a traditional, almost stereotypic attitude toward women. His preference is for his warm, maternal characters, women who exude strength and security and who are associated with the hearth and the home, whether they be his older "mother surrogates" or his young but precociously mature women like Molly and the matronly Emma. These are the women to whom his male characters are inevitably drawn, for they offer consultation when they are in doubt, consolation when they are in distress, and food when they are hungry.

These attributes are absent in the other types of women McMurtry portrays (they are never, for instance, portrayed in the context of a kitchen), who are usually seen as unhealthy for the protagonists; indeed, in some instances, they are overtly hostile and destructive. Examples are some of the minor characters, such as Charlene Duggs, the insensitive teenager who fails to give Sonny sexual satisfaction in *The Last Picture Show*, and the bevy of lesbians in *All My Friends Are Going To Be Strangers*, who are threatening to the male sexist Godwin and who act as a kind of witches' chorus in their hostile predictions for the future happiness of Danny Deck. One of them places a curse on Danny and predicts that he will be separated from his wife and all other women by an invisible pane of glass. The destructive women among the more major characters include Jacy Farrow *(The Last Picture Show)*, Sally Bynum and Jill Peel *(All My Friends Are Going To Be Strangers)*, Patsy Carpenter *(Moving On)*, and, to a certain extent, Eleanor Guthrie *(Moving On)*, and Lois Farrow *(The Last Picture Show)*. The younger females—Jacy, Sally, Jill, and Patsy—are emotionally immature, neurotic, egocentric; they seem incapable of loving the males who are attracted to them but contribute to their frustration and sense of isolation, while the mature and sexually emancipated females, such as Lois and Eleanor, scarred by emotional traumas in their past, reserve a "personal" area into which they can retreat and into which their lovers will never be allowed to enter, a defensive mechanism characterized by a certain reserve in their interpersonal relations with others.

Both Sonny and his best friend, Duane, are enamored of the vapid teenage narcissist Jacy Farrow. Their love for her strains their friendship and leads to frustration and unhappiness, for this small town succubus is destructive to both boys. Her teasing, flirtatious pitting of the two friends against each other succeeds in sending Duane off to the Korean War and Sonny to the hospital with the loss of an eye. Her callous handling of young male sensibility is epitomized in her brief and unconsummated marriage to Sonny. Appropriately, she, like Patsy Carpenter, is ultimately the recipient of what McMurtry must sense as poetic justice at the hands of a male chauvinist. Indeed, Abilene and Sonny Shanks are Texas machos who may be viewed as avatars of Hud in the role of sexual scourge or avenger who punish the shallow and selfish sexuality of Jacy and Patsy: Jacy is summarily discarded as a sex toy after her pool table seduction by Abilene, and, in *Moving On*, Patsy, instead of being ravished by Sonny Shanks, is hogtied like a young heifer and unceremoniously dumped in the rodeo pens at night.

If in her punishment by the personification of the male ego Patsy resembles Jacy Farrow, she exhibits even more similarities with Sally Bynum, who is neither as shallow as Jacy nor as unfeeling as Patsy but who shares the egocentricity common to both. Jacy is narcissistic in her lovemaking, which always has the aura of a theatrical performance with herself cast as star. She is a meretricious, dull, one-dimensional egoist. Sally, on the other hand, is a more interesting, if crueller, character in her amoral self-seeking. She uses Danny as a tool to accomplish her desires to bear a child; he is merely the seed bearer necessary for her impregnation, and when he has performed this function, she discards him without further thought.

Similarly, Patsy uses both her husband, Jim, and her lover, Hank, to satisfy her emotional needs. As a result, she causes them both a great deal of anxiety before she abandons them. Her emotional involvement with these two men is not terminated easily, however. Since Patsy is the protagonist of *Moving On*, the males in her life are contributory to her emotional development and maturation, a process fraught with much personal stress on Patsy's part. It is apparent that as Patsy "moves on" from her identity-seeking and troubled youth toward a maturer and wiser life as a divorced woman and mother, she will ultimately emerge as the emancipated loner, a type represented by Lois and Eleanor, rather than the warm women represented by McMurtry's maternal figures, for while Lois and Eleanor possess the admirable qualities of strength and endurance, they nevertheless remain, in their fierce independence, "takers" rather than "givers" (such as Molly, Ruth, Emma, or Genevieve). Patsy has learned from the example and thus will escape from the type, represented by the embittered, frustrated, and neurotic Lee

Duffin, who has become the cynical predator of young men. Similarly, her early shallowness has probably saved her from the frigid neuroticism of Jill Peel, who is so involved in her own unresolved crisis that she is unable to aid Danny in his. Danny loves Jill, but instead of salving his wounded sensibilities, she merely intensifies his feeling of rejection. Only the warm and giving maturer women—Emma, Jenny, and Juanita—can offer Danny temporary respite. This is not to say that Jill and Eleanor are to be equated with the totally unadmirable Jacy and Sally, but because they are caught up in their individual determinants, they cannot be the women that the McMurtry male needs. Jill is too weak and troubled herself to act as a psychological crutch for Danny, and Eleanor is too proud and independent to be the compliant female Sonny Shanks's ego demands or to sustain an interest in the adolescent affection felt for her by Jim Carpenter.

II *Adolescents*

McMurtry seems to have a particular aversion to the adolescent or immature male. Indeed, though the protagonists of his early fiction—Lonnie in *Horseman, Pass By*, Gid in the initial sections of *Leaving Cheyenne*, and Sonny in *The Last Picture Show*—are all adolescents who exhibit longing, indecision, and frustration, McMurtry's ultimate attitude toward them is unsympathetic. Lonnie is colorless in his groping immaturity and lack of sophistication; it is natural that the character of the mature if ruthless Hud overshadows the figure of the callow youth in the novel and becomes the title figure in the motion picture adaptation of the book. The director of *Hud*, Martin Ritt, cast Brandon de Wilde in the role of Lonnie, and de Wilde's performance fulfilled McMurtry's own realization of the character. In her review of the film, Pauline Kael observed that Brandon de Wilde's Lonnie was a "17-year-old blank sheet of paper" whose only "reality" stems from de Wilde's having played the role before: "from *Shane* to *Hud*, he has been our observer, our boy in the west, testing heroes."[13] McMurtry, observing de Wilde during location shots in Texas, says that it was clear that de Wilde "was struggling hard to leave adolescence behind, but it wasn't always clear whether he was winning or losing."[14]

Even when his male characters have left the precarious time of adolescence and have become, at least physiologically, adult men, they often remain psychologically fixed in an extended adolescence.

This is true of Gideon Fry, who remains an unhappy man because of the love he feels for Molly. Gid feels that because Molly does not marry him, he is destroyed, and he marries the wrong woman. McMurtry commented on Gid's attitude, remarking that to say that Molly destroyed Gid by refusing to marry him is to falsify the conditions of life. "He's a mature man," said McMurtry; "if she doesn't marry him it is still up to him to make his own life."[15]

Like Gid, Jim Carpenter in *Moving On* still exhibits an emotional immaturity after he is an adult, married male; indeed, one of the symptoms of Patsy Carpenter's emotional growth and maturity is her decision to terminate her marriage with him.

McMurtry has commented about the essential immaturity of all his male protagonists—even into adulthood:

Danny, as far as I'm concerned, is the first interesting young male I've done—if he *is* interesting at all. He's interesting to me. All the rest have been shadow figures—insubstantial, empty, just anonymous young males, really, not at all as vivid as the women. I think this is because I'm not interested in young men; I never have been. Insofar as I have been interested in men at all I'm interested in old men, like Sam and Roger, or eccentrics, like the screen writer and waifs, like Pee Wee, but I am really not interested in young men, and they are almost without exception my dullest and least vivid characters. If there is an exception it's Danny, he's more interesting than the young men in *The Last Picture Show* or *Horseman* or *Moving On*.[16]

McMurtry's reply to the question of why he found Danny Deck more interesting than Sonny Crawford in *The Last Picture Show* reveals a surprising antipathy for the character of Sonny. "That kid is a simple blank," he said. "I feel no emotion for him at all, no involvement with him at all, and I could hardly write the screen play because I felt so little for him. Peter [Bogdanovich] put in whatever was good about him in the movie—I thought of him as another slightly vapid high school kid." On the other hand, he said, Danny has "a lot more intensity, a lot more perception, a lot more originality, and, in many ways, a lot more character" than any of his other creations. Comparing Sonny and Danny, McMurtry said: "I don't think he [Danny] is at all adolescent; I think he is much more mature. He has insights and capacities that are far beyond anything that Sonny would ever have. Not that he is in complete control of his life, or in good control of it at all—he obviously is not. But capacity is more than control, and perception is a kind of capacity in itself."[17]

III *Cowboys and Rodeo Stars*

McMurtry, fascinated by the swaggering image of Lonnie's uncle, Hud Bannon, notes that the screenwriters for the movie version of the novel "had the good sense to shift the focus from Lonnie to Hud."[18] If in his ruthlessness and unbridled sexuality Hud is a prototype of Abilene in *The Last Picture Show* and Sonny Shanks in *Moving On*, he is also the archetype of the American mythic cowboy transposed to the mid-twentieth century. McMurtry writes that "insofar as he [Hud] has an archetypal or mythological dimension, he is not my creation but relates to that myth of the Westerner which the movies themselves have helped create." Nevertheless, Hud is a type rooted in reality. After seeing the film, many west Texans assured McMurtry that they knew someone just like Hud. "*Their* Hud was a real hellion, they told me—if they were men their tone indicated that he was the sort of man they almost wished they had been: tough, capable, wild, undomesticated."[19] McMurtry elaborated:

Hud, a twentieth-century westerner, is a gunfighter who lacks both guns and opponents. The land itself is the same—just as powerful, just as imprisoning—but the social context has changed so radically that Hud's impulse to violence has to turn inward on himself and his family. Hud Bannon is wild in a well-established tradition of western wildness that involves drinking, gambling, fighting, fast and reckless riding and/or driving (Hud has a Cadillac), and, of course, seducing. The tradition is not bogus; the character is pretty much in line with actuality. The cowboy, on screen and off, has generally been distinguished for his daring and his contempt of the middle-class way of life (he remains acutely conscious of the mores of his peers). Although nowadays most cowboys are solidly middle-class in their values, the values sit more lightly on them than on their white-collar cousins.[20]

Hud's Cadillac functions on both the literal and symbolic levels of the novel. As McMurtry indicates, Hud "is not simply a cowboy; if he were, he could never afford the Cadillac. It is his gun, in a sense, and he can afford it because he is the son of a well-to-do rancher, and a wheeler in his own right. . . . To a rancher, a Cadillac has a dual usefulness, just as the gunfighter's gun once had: it is an obvious and completely acceptable status symbol, and also it is capable of making the long, high-speed drives that frequently are necessary in cattle country; it will do the work."[21] The Cadillac is also a symbol of Hud's sexual prowess and is used in his escapades with Lily, the wife of Truman Peters.

Sonny Shanks's Cadillac hearses in *Moving On* function in a similar fashion: "For years Shanks had driven Cadillac hearses—they were an essential part of his legend. The hearses were white and he always had three sets of bulls' horns painted in gold on each one: a set on each door and one on the top, so people in airplanes would know it was him, he said. On occasions when he had to fly to make a rodeo he would hire a needy rookie to drive the hearse to him" (p. 36). The vehicles not only function as advertisements for the "World's Champion Cowboy" but also as mobile boudoirs; each hearse is stocked with liquor and outfitted with a bed in back.

On a less grandiose scale, Abilene's car serves a similar function in *The Last Picture Show*. The deep-throated sound of its twin exhaust pipes are heard by Lois Farrow as Abilene speeds away into the night after Jacy's seduction. Abilene drives a souped-up Mercury with gutted mufflers, and the car seems to symbolize his animality and seductiveness. In Thalia, the "sound of his exhausts was as unmistakable as the sound of the wind" (p. 6), and after he impulsively seduces Jacy and returns her to her home, he "raced his motor and made his mufflers roar, so that anyone in the neighborhood who was awake would know what car was in the driveway" before speeding off in the night (p. 220). There is nothing "vulgar" in the car, "no dice hanging from the rearview mirror," but one of the car's accoutrements indicates the owner's preoccupation with Eros; instead of the traditional dashboard Jesus or plastic figure of Mary, there is "a tiny, expensive-looking statue of a naked woman. A magnet held it to the dashboard, and as the car moved the statue wiggled provocatively. The woman had a gold stomach and tiny little bloodstones for nipples" (p. 216). The car is such an obvious sexual symbol that even sitting in it is seductive for the impressionable Jacy: "Just getting in the Mercury was exciting: it was the most famous car in that part of the country, and the seat covers smelled of tobacco and beer" (p. 216). Jacy, the thrill-seeking teenager of Thalia, is eroticized by the olfactory aspects of Abilene's mobile sex symbol; conversely, Patsy Carpenter, the young married Dallasite, is repulsed by the seminal smell of Sonny's wheeled bedroom/bar (*Moving On*, pp. 40–41, 43).

This freewheeling sexuality so closely associated with the characters of Hud, Abilene, and Sonny is only one aspect of the twentieth-century cowboy archetype McMurtry establishes in his fiction. "In addition to the wildness," writes McMurtry, "Hud also exhibits other characteristics which are typically cowboy: independence is first among them, then pride, stoicism, directness, restlessness. The cowboy also has his own astringent brand of humor". These characteristics are shared by all the cowboy archetypes in McMurtry's fiction, and all of them are seen to be struggling to retain an identity in a rigidly circumscribed and rapidly diminishing world that limits the possibilities for self-definition. "Hud Bannon's West," writes McMurtry, "is a sort of new lost frontier, and Hud is one of the many people whose capacities no longer fit his situation. He needs more room and less company, and he is unlikely to get either." If the temperament of the cowboy has not changed appreciably since the nineteenth century, his environment has "steadily shrunk." "There are no more trail herds, no more wide-open cattle towns; no more is there the vast stretch of unfenced land between Laredo and Calgary. If a cowboy is to be really footloose these days, he must take to the rodeo circuit."[22]

Even the possibilities of rodeoing are diminishing as the cowboy is gradually drawn toward the town, lessening considerably his isolation and diminishing "his sense of himself as a man alone."[23] Thus in *Moving On*, Pee Wee Raskin gradually gives up his notion of becoming a rodeo star as he is inevitably drawn back, time and time again, to the metropolitan sprawl of Houston. Here the displaced cowboy, still wearing his cowboy hat amid the urbanites, spends his days driving a miniature train in the city zoo and his nights in a disreputable lounge in southeast Houston. Similarly, when Pete Tatum gives up rodeoing to become a car salesman for his father-in-law in Fort Worth, he takes on the aspects of a beaten man: "he was not quite the same man" and "the heaviness of his face bespoke a sadness, a disappointment" (*Moving On*, p. 653). Although Patsy tries to cheer Pete up by saying rodeoing is "a ridiculous profession anyway, and you know it," Pete's demeanor belies her words. "He was dressed as she had always seen him dressed, in Levi's and a faded Western shirt. It was hard to imagine him in a white shirt, a tie and cheap suit, standing on a windy lot in Fort Worth. It would only be dull for him, and empty, and the dullness and emptiness were already settling in his face" (p. 654). Marrying and settling down had removed Pete from so much that was a part of him: "The West, all that country, those drives he and Boots loved, and rodeo, horses, and bulls, the whole movement of the arena. For all that it was dumb and dull to her, it kindled something vital in Pete. He matched with it in some way. So did Sonny. Even Pee Wee matched with it, in his way. On the zoo train he was just a sad uneducated kid in a big city, doing a silly job. Pete would look just as sad on a car lot, it seemed to her. It had already taken something from him. He no longer looked like a man who could move faster than a bull" (p. 654).

Significantly, Sonny Shanks's feeling that he is getting too old to rodeo signals his death. While in Las Vegas to judge a Miss Rodeo America pageant, he telephones his mistress, Eleanor, and says, "I was just thinking, maybe what I need to do is let my hair grow and take lots of speed and LSD and turn into a cowboy hippie. Maybe it ain't too late for me yet. I could sort of be the Joe Namath of rodeo, you know" (p. 660). Finally he decides to marry Eleanor and settle down on her immense ranch. Before returning to Texas and a re- tired life with his aging millionairess, however, he drives to Los Angeles to retrieve his championship saddle, which he had left behind. The saddle, with its golden horn, symbolizes Sonny's mas- culinity as well as his ability in the arena. When Jim Carpenter defends Sonny to Patsy he says, "After all, he's been World's Champion Cowboy three times. That saddle in the hearse was a championship saddle." Patsy replies, "That wasn't a saddle. It was an altar. I bet he deflowers a virgin on it every week" (p. 43).

Sonny's dicision to drive to Los Angeles to get his championship saddle causes his death. Speeding into Los Angeles in his hearse, Sonny collides first with an old Buick full of hippies and then is struck by a Chrysler driven by a swinger from Van Nuys: "It was not as wrecks go on that freeway, a very disastrous wreck. The hearse hit a spot in the traffic and it was late enough that the pile-up was not bad. Only nine cars were involved. Three people were hurt seriously but not as seriously as they might have been, and of the fourteen people injured only one, Sonny Shanks, World's Cham- pion Cowboy, was killed" (p. 667).

Whether it be the slow, psychologically wasting death of Pee Wee on his miniature train and Pete on his used car lot, or the quick and violent death of Sonny in the swirl of freeway traffic, McMurtry sees the city as being inimical to the cowboy. "Someday," writes McMurtry, "the ranches of America will all be Southern California size, and all the cattle, perhaps, will be grown in the great feedlots of the Middle West. The descendants of the trail hands will be driving beer trucks in the suburbs of San Antonio, Dodge City, Cheyenne, and a hundred other towns whose names once held a different promise."[24]

McMurtry has described a synthetic rodeo he saw in Madison Square Garden:

> Behind the chutes were passages leading down into the concrete bowels of the Garden: to descend would have removed one completely from the scene of the action, and anyway the prospect seemed a little Dantesque. . . . The cowboys seemed to feel the same way; they huddled as close to the arena as possible. I noticed a number of them cleaning their fingernails, which is what cowboys always do when they feel vulnerable and at a loss. They were cut off from their culture, and had neither sky above nor land below; the only honest soil around was under their fingernails.[25]

He thinks that the rodeo riders have already sold out to the cities and "that whether they like it or not, they are in show business, and their work is in the towns, not on the land." He attacks the romanticized view of the rodeo hand, a view promulgated by such movies as *Junior Bonner*, *J. W. Coop*, and *The Honkers*, that the men who "drag along from rodeo to rodeo, barely making their entry fees," do so because it is the only "free way of life open to them." This view springs from the myth created by movies and books about the West, a myth that sees the drifter as the embodiment of frontier individualism and glorifies him at the expense of the settler: "The drifter-figure has come to represent for us all that was romantic and free about the West, the settler all that is bourgeois, stable and dull" (pp. 60–61).

McMurtry feels that the cattleman's rather contemptuous view of the rodeo hand is accurate. To them the rodeo hands are "preeminently accommodationists, modern men who hold themselves responsible only to the demands of their egos, men who take no care of the land itself and have no respect for the labors or the traditions of the herdsman." This view of the rodeo cowboy, says McMurtry, has no mythic or aesthetic appeal, "but then these men do not deserve to be glorified as holdouts against a system which they use and cater to every day" (p. 61).

The true holdouts against the system, McMurtry feels, are the embittered farmers and stockmen whose lives have not been a series of changes in women, horses, and locales. "These are men, for the most part, who have lived in one place, loved the West and its ideals, and increased only in despair—as the oil industry ruined their grass, as the air and water grew foul, as the land taxes rose so high they could not afford to stock their acreage, as their life-styles were scorned and then parodied, their children drawn away to the cities and there subverted." These are the men who served as models for Homer Bannon in *Horseman, Pass By*, Gideon Fry and his father in *Leaving Cheyenne*, Sam the Lion in *The Last Picture Show*, and Roger Waggoner in *Moving On*. They are men who, despite a world of changing values, indeed, perhaps because of it, can lead lives of what McMurtry calls "a moral and physical astringency" and exhibit the qualities of honesty, bravery, endurance, dignity, nobility, and, most importantly in the creation of mythic or epic figures, tragedy:

Real cattle people are sad now, with something of the sadness of gorillas. Like gorillas they may become truculent and make noise to scare interlopers away, but in reality they are a breed in retreat, with a deeply ingrained sense of their doom. Only when you see them on the remoteness of ranches, far from towns and crowds and hoopla, do they show themselves as men of wit and grace, playfulness and occasional nobility; though sad, it is not altogether to be lamented that so many of them have been kept from prosperity, for if one thing is evident about cowboys it is that they are men who show their best qualities only under the worst of natural conditions. It is poverty and drought, isolation and toil that bring out their richest humor and strongest loyalty, their deepest feeling for nature and their keenest joy in life. Give them money and creature comforts, and everything that is lean, well-crafted, enduring and humanly beautiful in them disappears and they quickly degenerate into mindless and tasteless suburbanized slobs.[26]

Hud's callousness, his lack of the old values subscribed to by Homer Bannon, are at least partially caused by his gradual "suburbanization" as he assimilates (and is assimilated by) a culture alien to Homer. Similarly, the attitudes toward adultery that so alienated Jimmy, the son of Molly and Gid in *Leaving Cheyenne*, would be totally foreign to the urbanized and college-bred Jim and Hank in

Moving On. Roger Waggoner is uneasy in the alien air of metropolitan Houston when he comes to visit Patsy and her baby shortly before his death, Pee Wee Raskin is an absurd incongruity among the denizens of the urban dives, Hank Malory is awkward and out of place in a midtown university, and Pete Tatum will suffer spiritual as well as physical dislocation confined to the asphalt paving of a used car lot in suburban Fort Worth. To transplant men who are so deeply rooted in the soil of the open plains to the hostile environment of the urban sprawl is to precipitate their spiritual, if not their literal, death. It is symbolic as well as ironic that the World's Champion Cowboy plunges to his death not astride a horse but in a hearse on an elevated Los Angeles freeway. Writing of this displacement of body and dislocation of spirit in the introduction to *In a Narrow Grave*, McMurtry says that it is the "movement, from country to subdivision, homeplace to metropolis, that gives life in present-day Texas its passion. Or if not its passion, its strong, peculiar mixture of passions, part spurious and part genuine, part ridiculous and part tragic"(p. xv).

IV   The Texas Rangers

McMurtry's characters are, for the most part, presented realistically; however, when he deals with recognizable types for which he has a deep-rooted antipathy, the characterization often borders on the grotesque. This is particularly true in *The Last Picture Show* where the portraits of the high school beauty queen, Jacy Farrow, the studiedly masculine (but latently homosexual) football coach, Herman Popper, and the religious fanatic, Brother Blanton, are carried past stereotype and into caricature by the intensity of McMurtry's scorn.

The characterization of E. Paul and Luther, the two brutal Texas Rangers who stop Danny and Petey on a back country road in *All My Friends Are Going To Be Strangers*, might appear to be caricature to some readers; actually, the personality and actions of the two men represent realism at its rawest. In "Southwestern Literature?" an essay in *In a Narrow Grave*, McMurtry spends six pages criticizing Walter Prescott Webb's sentimentalized portrait of the Rangers in *The Texas Rangers*. Webb's inordinate admiration of the Rangers, writes McMurtry, caused him to whitewash them in a book filled with "hero worship." Although Thomas Landess has suggested that

McMurtry is excessive in his criticism of Webb's idealization of the Rangers, it is obvious from both his nonfiction and fiction that McMurtry has a personal conviction about the organization.[27] His portraits of Luther and E. Paul were not an attempt to demythify the idolization of the Rangers, however:

[The characterization] is pretty much based on personal experience. Not that I have been personally brutalized by Rangers—but I have observed many Rangers, and a good bit of their behavior, and I think it is pretty brutal, essentially. I am not sure that that is the way to demythicize them, I think that is only in a sense the backside of the myth of the Rangers anyway. I just meant it as a fairly realistic example. I've always disliked them, and I've known some, and I feel that their situations, if anything, makes them more brutal than they would incline to be otherwise. It is a cultivated brutality, almost. They are maintaining a status quo that is essentially lost but that they have to emphasize in order to continue to exist.[28]

CHAPTER 5

McMurtry and the Motion Pictures

THE careers of few contemporary American novelists have been as intimately associated with motion pictures as that of Larry McMurtry. An ardent film buff, McMurtry has written film scripts and film criticism and has begun a book on his experiences with cinema.[1] Three of McMurtry's novels—*Horseman, Pass By* (1961), *Leaving Cheyenne* (1962), and *The Last Picture Show* (1966)—have been adapted to the screen, and options have been purchased on *All My Friends Are Going To Be Strangers* (the motion picture adaptations of *Horseman, Pass By* and *The Last Picture Show* won Academy Awards). Reference to movies and to movie makers are frequent in *Moving On* and *All My Friends Are Going To Be Strangers*, and motion pictures and the local movie house are central to the plot of *The Last Picture Show.*

I Hud: *The Western Antihero*

McMurtry is not fond of the motion picture *Hud,* but he exhibits the same attitude toward *Horseman, Pass By,* the novel on which the film was based. He has written that Paul Newman and Patricia Neal "took advantage of their roles as brilliantly as the camera took advantage of the terrain; between them they saved what was otherwise a weak and badly shaped dramatic vehicle."[2] McMurtry had nothing to do with the script of *Hud,* and although he feels that the screen writers had "the good sense" to shift the emphasis from the character of Lon to that of Hud, they generally followed the book and "as a result most of the confusion and all of the sentimentality were carried over" into the film.[3] In retrospect, McMurtry wishes he had made Hud the central character in the novel. The shift in the movie version was natural, he said, because in the movies the emphasis is always on the stronger male character,

87

particularly under the star system. "That's how they had to cast the picture, and finance the picture. That part had to be built up, it was natural, and if I were writing the book today that's the way I would write it."[4]

Martin Ritt, the director of *Hud*, consistently emphasized the moral and ethical contrast between Homer Bannon (played by veteran actor Melvyn Douglas) and his rapacious stepson, Hud (played by Paul Newman). Newman dominated every scene in which he appeared, and although most critics eulogized Douglas's patrician characterization of Homer, McMurtry agreed with Pauline Kael, who alone among the major critics preferred Paul Newman's role of Hud to Melvyn Douglas's portrayal of the noble rancher. Kael finds Douglas's Homer as "prating and tedious as Polonius,"[5] and McMurtry writes that "old Homer collapsed as pathetically and unconvincingly in the movie as he had in the book."[6]

Pauline Degenfelder has suggested that a conscious use of animal imagery in both the novel and the film offers a further contrast between Homer and Hud. She argues that in both *Horseman, Pass By* and *Hud*, the animal references to Homer "signify his sympathetic response to nature, a trait reinforced by his refusal to drill for oil on his land":

> In his preface to *In a Narrow Grave*, McMurtry states that in former times the horseman was "the god of the country;" hence, Homer's nickname, "Wild Horse," indicates his legendary status, which even the cynical Hud recognizes. Homer's parallels with the longhorn cattle sharpen his character: like Homer the longhorns are the foundation of the ranch and a remembrance of times past. When Homer states that "them big horns'll never go through a chute," he is describing his disability to be circumscribed by the limitations—legal, geographical, and moral—of an encroaching society. The novel's animal references to minor characters are diminished in the film and increased at Hud's expense, where they are usually degrading. . . . His use of technology for the abuse of nature is underlined when, in violation of both manmade laws and ecological balance, Hud kills the buzzards that are feeding on the infected carcass. In the novel this action is performed by a minor character, and its assignment to Hud in the film defines him as an alien presence in nature.[7]

Although Homer is often filmed astride his horse, Hud is seen only once on horseback. "His emblem," says Degenfelder, "is the Cadillac," which crushes Alma's flowers, (Halmea is called Alma in the movie adaptation). His reckless driving has been the cause of his brother's death and almost the cause of Homer's. Degenfelder points out that animal references to Hud are intensified in the film through the visuals, for example, in his juxtaposition with the long horns mounted on the wall, symbolizing his sexual appetite and prowess. The pig-catching contest also serves a symbolic purpose:

Hud says, "I wouldn't want to be hoggish," but his actions belie his words. His greed marks such minor incidents as his appropriating an opponent's pig, Lon's ice cream, and another man's wife, and reaches a crescendo in his attempts to rape Alma and to seize his father's land. The desecration of the earth goddess Alma is paralleled by Hud's plan to defile the land with oil rigs. Both actions signify his antipathy to nature, his departure from the attitudes of classic Western heroes, and his role as ironic protagonist.[8]

McMurtry says Hud "is essentially the creation of the film. Insofar as he has an archetypal or mythological dimension, he is not my creation but relates to that myth of the Westerner which the movies themselves have helped create."[9] McMurtry has always been interested in the mythic aspects of the West, particularly those formed by the Western movie. Indeed, he has collaborated on a film script with Peter Bogdanovich that was to be "a Western about the end of the West." The plan was to cast John Wayne, James Stewart, and Henry Fonda in the film and to utilize the traditions and myths these men had created as Western actors—"the tradition they had established as Western actors as embodiment of the Western myth, brought to a culmination."[10] The actors, says McMurtry, did not like the idea—"they didn't want the West to end, they didn't want to be old men"—and refused to participate in the film. Without their cooperation, the movie will probably never be produced. The roles were written with these three actors in mind, and the film was to be a "beautiful, bittersweet story about three old men having their last adventure after which everything is sort of all over—for them and the West. Without these actors the movie would not be the same. We could do it with unknown people or character actors and it might even be more honest, but it wouldn't have that kind of mythic resonance of those faces you've seen so many times before—connected with the past of the West."[11]

II *The Movies in McMurtry's Fiction*

The movie industry plays an important role in *Moving On.* Patsy Carpenter, the protagonist of the book, finds a sympathetic confidante in Joe Percy, a Hollywood screenwriter. Patsy's husband, Jim, works briefly for the movie industry in Texas and later in Hollywood; Eleanor Guthrie's lover, the cowboy rodeo star Sonny Shanks, is also associated with the movies before his death in Los Angeles; and much of the action of the novel centers around the filming of location shots in Texas for a film about rodeos.

Danny Deck, the protagonist of *All My Friends Are Going To Be Strangers*, also has many associations with movies, the movie industry, those who work for the industry, and those who would like to work for it. One of his acquaintances in Houston is an eccentric janitor who works the night shift in the university library and who wants desperately to become a screenwriter:

Henry had been wanting to get in pictures for about fifteen years, and had taken to calling Zanuck almost every night. He never got past the outermost answering service, but he was convinced it was because Zanuck was so busy. He had written eight strange screen plays, all of them involving the Seventh Cavalry—in the most bizarre of them the Seventh Cavalry only barely managed to keep the Flathead Indians from razing San Francisco, which Henry had resituated somewhere near Portland, to save shooting costs, he said. [pp. 28–29]

When Danny's first novel is accepted for motion picture adaptation, he moves to California where he meets Hollywood eccentrics such as Leon O'Reilly and the strange Jill Peel, an animated cartoon artist with whom he falls in love (on their first night together, they watch an old movie, *Viva Zapata*, on television). The last person that Danny talks to in the end of the novel is a fugitive from the movie world, Peter Paul Neville, who attempts to prevent Danny from walking into the river.

Danny Deck has a preference for bad films, which he watches throughout *All My Friends:*

. . . when I gave up on my novel for the day I could drift down to Market Street and pick out a couple of movies and forget things for a while. I can watch any movie, and I averaged one or two a day all the time I was in San Francisco. . . . I never went to the art films that were always being shown—I only went to the third rate movies on Market Street. I didn't want to see films that reminded me about life—I wanted to see films that bore little relation to it: Italian spectacles, horror movies, comedies, anything unreal. I was escaping from reality for a couple of hours, and wanted the escape to be as pure and complete as possible. I could always have reality—it was all around me. [p. 91]

Like his creation, Danny Deck, McMurtry prefers third-rate films, and also like Danny, he often sees them in abundance. In the passage quoted above, Danny indicates that he saw two movies a day during his stay in San Francisco, but McMurtry has beat this record. On a marathon movie-viewing experience, he writes: "I hied myself to Times Square "and saw seventeen movies more or less right after the other. I say more or less because there was a gap of some seven hours, between 4 and 11 A.M., when the Times Square theaters were closed." McMurtry spent the time while the theaters were closed watching "the Late Late Late TV Movie, in this case *Istanbul.*"[12]

McMurtry defends his preference for bad movies: "The lessons to be learned from bad movies he says, are many and varied, but *sic transit* is first among them." A film such as *Istanbul,* for instance, gives one "views of mortality more distinct and more unnerving than anything to be found in serious films." The strength and radiance of great movies contradict mortality: "great images of suffering always seem to ennoble the poor human subject who is doing the suffering, and even humiliation can be dignified by good direction—as witness *Umberto D.*" He avoids good movies because they depress him; "Good movies press upon one, much like Reality, and I will do almost anything to escape them." "Personally," he continues, "I know that when I disappear for a weekend into bad movies I am not seeking either truth or art, but am handing both a flat rejection."[13]

Movies are essential to the plot and to the theme of *The Last Picture Show.* The teenagers of Thalia, for instance, draw their personal icons and their sexual referents from the movies. McMurtry said about this phenomenon: "The movie is about the only art form accessible to someone who's stuck out in the middle of West Texas in a small town. There are no theatres, no adequate libraries. What is there besides the movie? Movies are one's contact with the world of the imagination. With romance. They are the only thing which offers one any concept of masculinity or femininity which serve as an alternative to the one the town offers: the football player and the high school beauty queen."[14]

In *The Last Picture Show* the passion of Sonny Crawford's girl friend, Charlene Duggs, is inextricably linked to the motion pictures. She was "always getting worked up in picture shows; at first Sonny had thought her fits of cinematic passion very encouraging, until he discovered it was practically impossible to get her worked up *except* in picture shows" (p. 18). The "movies were Charlene's life," and she spends most of her afternoons in her mother's beauty shop reading movie magazines. She always refers to movie stars by their first names, has her bedroom full of dime store portraits of Hollywood stars, and sleeps with a picture of Van Johnson under her pillow. In one of their lovemaking sessions, Charlene and Sonny are necking during a screening of *Storm Warning*, which stars Steve Cochran and Ginger Rogers. Charlene imagines that Sonny looks "a little bit like Steve Cochran," and the thought makes her begin to "kiss him energetically, squirming and pressing herself against his knee" (p. 18). Sonny responds with divided attention, keeping one eye on the screen, for the posters outside the movie house showed Ginger Rogers in a slip, and if she suddenly "decided to take her clothes off he didn't want to miss it." Here, as elsewhere, McMurtry's movie viewers prefer their fantasies to their realities.

Like Sonny and Charlene, Duane and Jacy utilize the intimate darkness of the movie house for their passionate embraces, and, like Charlene, Jacy becomes more amorous when movie images pervade her lovemaking. She likes to kiss Duane while sitting in the dim light of a tiny overhead bulb at the back of the school bus. The orange glow of the bulb was "romantic and suggestive," lending an aura of theatricality to the kissing "scenes" of Jacy and Duane while the "audience" of classmates makes Jacy feel like a movie star. Duane is totally unprepared for the shock he receives when Jacy abruptly terminates their romance. He had expected a Hollywood ending to their affair; "you were supposed to get whoever you really loved. That was the way it worked in movies" (p. 188).

The sexual fantasies of Thalia's teenage boys incorporate the images of screen actresses, and when they have actual sexual experiences, they find that they compare unfavorably with their fantasies. When Sonny begins his affair with the aging wife of his football coach, he notes that she is "not as pretty as a movie star" (p. 121), and the boys who hire an ugly whore for a sexual escapade have always imagined sex "in terms of pretty girls, movie stars like Elizabeth Taylor" (p. 109).

The closing of the movie house after the screening of the last picture show, *The Kid from Texas*, symbolizes on one level the termination of a phase in the life of the book's protagonist as he moves from the uncertainty of adolescence to the loneliness of maturity. Even the title of the novel utilizes an allusion to the movies.

III   *McMurtry as Script Writer*

The Last Picture Show had its genesis in McMurtry's bitter experience of a three-day return visit to his home in Archer City in 1965. McMurtry wrote the novel in six weeks while the mood of pique was still upon him. By the time the book was published in 1966, however, he realized that it was "too bitter" and that he had been unfair to his hometown. In a review of the movie version of the novel, he wrote: "Archer City had not been cruel to me, only honestly indifferent, and my handling of many of the characters in the book represented a failure of generosity for which I blame no one but myself."[15]

The film script, the result of a close collaboration between McMurtry and the film director, Peter Bogdanovich, is a much more sympathetic portrait of McMurtry's hometown than is the novel (Archer City, called Thalia in the novel, is called Anarene in the film). The combination of the two young writers was fortunate. McMurtry felt at once that Bogdanovich had a sense of the 1950's, the time of the novel's setting. More importantly, however, he had what McMurtry terms an "elegiac sense," and this, feels McMurtry, is what made the film a triumph. "He is moved, as I am, by the ending of things, by the waning of periods, generations, human couples, a town. I might have deduced this from his feeling for Ford and Hawks, the most elegiac of our directors, but such is the piece-meal nature of film work that I didn't sense it fully until I saw the finished picture." McMurtry says that the novel had not been entirely unsympathetic, but that "a certain amount of affection struggled in it, and a certain amount of genuine hatred. Affection lost, and the predominant tone of the novel is rather harshly satiric."[16] He believes that Bogdanovich approached the material more objectively and more sympathetically than he did.

The filmed version of *The Last Picture Show* established Peter Bogdanovich as an important film director. Most critics saw the film's recreation of the 1950's as an example of authentic Americana and of life-styles and attitudes that had almost completely passed from the national consciousness. Vincent Canby, reviewing the film for the *New York Times*, pointed out that *The Last Picture Show* delineates a time "when television was taking hold of the land, when movie theatres were closing by the thousands, and when Americans were giving up one more contact with the communities in which they lived" (4 Oct. 1971). The visuals of the film superbly support this passing of a way of life: the opening shot in the film shows the town's single movie house where the populace gathered their dreams. The camera then pans up the tawdry and dreary main street of Anarene. The last shot of the film reverses the opening, the camera ending with a shot of the closed theater after the last picture show has played. In the novel the two movies that Sonny and Duane attend are *Storm Warning* and *The Kid from Texas*. The film alters these to *Father of the Bride* and *Red River*. Bogdanovich explained the substitution of *Red River* for *The Kid from Texas* by saying, "I wanted the theater to go out with a bang. I wanted [the film] to be—in counterpoint—a Western about the beginning of things." Actually, the substitution may have been suggested by the novel itself; Sonny and Duane are disappointed in the last movie playing before the theater closes, for "it would have taken *Winchester '73* or *Red River* or some big movie like that to have crowded out the memories the boys kept having" (p. 265).

If, as Bogdanovich suggests, *Red River* is a Western about beginnings, then the McMurtry-Bogdanovich film is a Western about endings: the end of adolescence, symbolized by the coming of age of Sonny and Duane; the end of innocence, symbolized by the death of Billy; the end of integrity and morality in a morass of hypocrisy and amorality, symbolized by the death of Sam the Lion,[17] the end of a love affair, outlined in the soliloquies of Sam and Lois; the end of happiness, symbolized in Ruth Popper's realization that Sonny will leave her again. Indeed, the decay of the town after the death of Sam the Lion and the closing of the movie house may be seen to signal the end of the American dream. As Lois Farrow muses in the film, "nothin's ever the way it's supposed to be." Perhaps it is this sense of something lost—youth, a way of life, the American dream—that makes the movie so popular. McMurtry writes that "its success in the highly urban areas where it is being shown convinces one more than ever that we live in a zombie-state these days; people respond to *The Last Picture Show* partly because it reminds them of how it was in the days when they felt."[18]

McMurtry feels that the last scene in the film (one that Bogdanovich retained despite some pressures to cut it) is the finest, for without it the film would have "no bottom, no fullness, no real dimension":

A boy comes back to an aging woman, herself hopelessly married. He has left her for a pretty face; the pretty face dropped him; his friend is sent to

Korea; another friend is killed; alone, he comes back to the woman he hurt. She hates him, she explodes, but then, nonetheless, knowing she is foolish, knowing in a matter of months or years he will leave her again for another pretty face, or she will grow too old, or something will happen to destroy them, she finds the fact that she can feel more important than anything that has happened or can happen—in brief, that feeling outweighs the inevitability and pain of its own extinction—and she takes him back. It leaves us, not just with a movie about defeat, but with a movie about living-in-spite-of-or-in-the-teeth-of-defeat, a superb thing for any work of art to try to be about. The woman is not smart or optimistic, she is just brave in relation to her life, as are several of the people in the film, for courage, humor, even gaiety in the face of bleakness and nothingness is not just engaging, it is compelling, and it is perhaps the cruciality of this unending conflict between love of life and despair in living, dramatized against the powerfully empty Texas landscape, that makes people leave *The Last Picture Show* feeling they have been hit where they least expected to be hit by a current movie—namely in the gut.[19]

McMurtry's review of the movie *The Last Picture Show* for the *Colonial Times* was followed by his defense of the film in *The Daily Rag* against the "radico-Sapphic" critique of Rita Mae Brown. Brown had seen a sexist or male chauvinist bias in the film. McMurtry responds, however, that he didn't claim "manhood" in "any admirable sense of the word" for anyone but Sam the Lion, and

he achieved it, if he did, after much personal tragedy: the loss of three sons, his wife's insanity, the marriage (to a lesser man) of a woman he loved, etc. . . . The Coach is shown to be a monster of boorish indifference; Gene Farrow is an obviously weak bore; Abilene no more than a small town cocksman. The boys do not grow up. Sonny is never more the lost boy than in the last scene—pathetic not tragic, and pathetic because we can see that he is never going to get beyond the view of manhood that the town offers him: a view that limits manhood to the prowess of a high school athlete.

Brown also attacked McMurtry as a denigrator of women, but McMurtry counters that all the adult women are shown to be "larger, more generous, more intelligent, and more courageous than their men." The inadequacies of the males, says McMurtry, are pointed up constantly, while the strength of the women is exalted: "Genevieve is supporting her family, Lois is trying to make Jacy into an intelligent woman, Ruth tries to make Sonny into someone more sensitively manly than the slob who wrecked her own life."[20]

IV McMurtry's Film Criticism

McMurtry's defense of the screen adaptation of *The Last Picture Show* in the *Colonial Times* and *The Daily Rag* shows a developing film aesthetic that had begun with his early essay "Cowboys, Movies, Myths, and Cadillacs" published in *Man and the Movies* in 1967 and that was continued in a *New York* magazine essay, "Movie-Tripping," in 1973.[21] In its defense of "bad" cinematic art, "Movie-Tripping" makes some important observations about the largely working-class audiences who view these films and who prefer "spectacle" to "art." The analysis of the middle-class couples who see such hard-core pornography as *Deep Throat* is also interesting. This essay indicates the type of film critique that can be expected in the monograph on film that McMurtry plans to write, a project that grew out of his plan to write a long essay about his experiences as a screenwriter:

I got started on an essay which grew out of an invitation from the *Times* to do a guest review. Instead of doing the review I spent a weekend "movie-tripping" and saw seventeen movies. In writing about this experience (they were all bad movies) and attempting to decide why I generally prefer bad movies to good movies I have gotten into a book on my whole experience as a film watcher and writer. Half of the book will be about myself as a watcher, and half as a writer. I will do it after I finish the novel [the third of the trilogy that includes *Moving On* and *All My Friends Are Going To Be Strangers*]. It will be short, only about 150 pages—sort of an extended essay.

An important example of McMurtry's film criticism is a review of *Lovin' Molly*, the movie based on his second novel, *Leaving Cheyenne*.[22] The review is totally negative in its appraisal of Sidney Lumet's film. By the time McMurtry wrote the article, he had cooled considerably in his earlier attitude toward *Leaving Cheyenne*, for he found the novel's vision of "adult life in which sexuality cannot seriously interfere with friendship" immature, sentimental, unrealistic, and dangerous. Lumet, says McMurtry, "dwelt lovingly on every sentimentality and every piece of poetic wishful thinking I was capable of at 22." Yet it is not for the acceptance of his own youthful fantasy that McMurtry attacks Lumet but for the total disregard of realism in setting and characterization and, most importantly, for Lumet's lack of fidelity to a tradition that is dying. McMurtry says that he is writing "not as an embittered author, but as an annoyed native": "The book I wrote is only vulnerable to its own flaws, but the tradition I am heir to is vulnerable to all sorts of demoralizations; it is a tradition that has already lost confidence in itself to such an extent that the people who remain in it have begun to look to its interpreters to tell them not only what they are but what they were. Tackiness, laziness, and poor craftsmanship on the part of the interpreters can only speed the demoralization."[23]

It becomes clear that McMurtry is judging Lumet's work not only aesthetically (from the standpoint of movie making) but morally (from the standpoint of a violated tradition). "There is no reason, of course," says McMurtry, "why Lumet should know that tradition, love it, or even be mildly interested in it; what one would have hoped is that he would take his own work seriously enough either to develop some interest and inform himself about the texture of regional life, or else simply pass the project and let the region alone." McMurtry argues that it was not the author of *Leaving Cheyenne* but rather the people of Bastrop, Texas, that deserved a better film treatment. Here McMurtry reveals the same ambivalence toward the region, the town, and the townspeople that was evidenced in *The Last Picture Show.*

Mr. Lumet took a place that was awful to begin with, but authentically awful, at least, and he antiqued it and rinky-dinked around with it until whatever bleak dignity it could claim was coated in a sticky, sugary falsity; instead of producing a work that would, in a modest way, have helped people recognize themselves, he has, perhaps more out of indifference than ineptitude, produced a grotesque distortion, and erected yet another small barrier to any meaningful or moving recognition. One cannot but think it a shame.[24]

The stance McMurtry assumed is further evidence of his insistence that when moviemakers depart from the purely escapist mode, they must observe fidelity to the subject being treated in their films—not only in the visuals but also in any subliminal comment conveyed by their medium. He objects to the romanticized image of the rodeo rider in recent Hollywood films. McMurtry notes that "*Junior Bonner, J. W. Coop,* the *Honkers* and the two or three other examples of the film industry's recent and unfortunate little love affair with rodeo are so alike thematically as to lead one to believe that in rodeo there is one story and one story only. This is the story of Odysseus the Wanderer as hard-up-aging small town rodeo hand."[25] McMurtry then proceeds to point out the many inaccuracies in the cinematic apotheosis of the rodeo hand.

McMurtry has examined at length another aspect of the world of motion pictures, screenwriting, in an eight-part series of essays published in *American Film*. The essays are autobiographical as well as critical. In the first, McMurtry examines screenwriting, which he considers a "craft" rather than an art. People have assumed that screenwriting is an art, "which needs to employ imaginative artists rather than a craft, which could be expected to rely upon the discipline and the trained skill of gifted artisans," an assumption that has led the motion picture industry to look outside its own ranks, "usually to novelists, for whatever writing it needs done." Conversely, no training of an indigenous corps of skilled craftsmen has taken place, so that "of the many crafts necessary to the making of motion pictures, that of the screenwriter is easily the most haphazard, the most impressionistic, and the most vulnerable."[26] Furthermore, continues McMurtry, screenwriting at present "has no rationale, no theory, and, at best, an indifferent, pedestrian craft-literature." Ultimately, he contends, the blame for this situation must be placed on the industry itself.

In "The Hired Pen," McMurtry humorously writes of the problems that beset a screenwriter from the moment of his initial contact by the studio, particularly those caused by the industry's expectation that the writer works purely out of love, with no consideration of the money he will gain from the project.

Producers are extremely reluctant to concede that money alone can be both an adequate and an honorable stimulus to an artist—and yet they are constantly put in the position of having to hope that it is. Stars and directors can be offered fame, but—except for the opportunity of working with stars and directors—money is all a producer can offer a screenwriter. Scarcely a handful of the thousands of writers who have worked in Hollywood have achieved either fame or creative satisfaction from doing so. What producers fail to recognize is that money sometimes activates, as nothing else can, a writer's sense of responsibility—even his sense of craft.[27]

McMurtry writes of other problems confronting the novelist who becomes a screenwriter for Hollywood in the next essay in his series, "The Deadline Syndrome." He again alludes to his distaste for *The Last Picture Show* and says that he was surprised that such a good film could be made from it. He theorizes that the novel was "exactly the kind of novel from which good movies are made—that is, a flatly written book with strong characterizations and a sense of period and place. Films like *The Blue Angel, Jules and Jim*, and *Treasure of Sierra Madre* were made from just such books—books that offer a director no stylistic resistance whatever. Towering classics always have a style and adapting them is like attempting to translate poetry, only more difficult."[28]

In "The Telephone Booth Screenwriter," McMurtry examines what he considers to have "engendered most of the misery writers have experienced in Hollywood, and thus most of the bitterness they harbor toward the movie industry": the Hollywood dictum that insists writers should be locally available. Having the writer "handy" allows for the possibility of inserting any newly hatched studio "idea" into the writer's emerging script. Prior to the 1960's, says McMurtry, half of the writers resident in Hollywood were there against their wills. "All of them had been uprooted from wherever their homes happened to be and brought into a more or less luxurious exile—and writers enjoy exile about as much as kings seem to. Some of the writers were allowed to bring their families with them, but this scarcely helped matters, since it meant that several people were uprooted and disoriented instead of just one."[29] McMurtry proposes an alternative based on the compromise that he himself effected with the studio when he worked with Peter Bogdanovich on the script of *The Last Picture Show*, a combination of daily posting of completed pages of script, a series of long-distance calls, and two trips to Hollywood for final consultations on the shooting script.

In "Personal Factors," McMurtry outlines the adjustments a novelist must make when shifting from fiction writing to screenwriting. "A writer who decides to do screenwork," says McMurtry, "should envision himself from the outset in the Balzacian or Dickensian mode—a man too big to boggle at details, rushing his sheets off to the printer with reckless abandon." A writer like Flaubert, with his commitment to the *mot juste*, contends McMurtry, will never be able to make the transition to the medium of movie writing, "a form in which no *mots* and few concepts are sacrosanct." The screenwriter must learn to be flexible to cope with the inevitable happenstance that characterizes the cinema: "personal accident,

executive whim, or simple limitations of time and money can combine to shatter even the most crystalline concept."[30]

McMurtry somewhat cynically dismisses writers who bemoan
their experience as screenwriters in "The Fun of It All." Though
these writers never claim that screenwriting is difficult, they inevitably feel that it is depressing work because of the Hollywood at-
mosphere or the stifling aura of the studio system. "What this boils
down to," says McMurtry, is that the writers somehow feel "mistreated, their genius slighted, degraded, or ignored." The real problem, he opines, is that the reality of screenwriting has not been
commensurate with their expectations, and in his view the reality of
the Hollywood scene can be enjoyed by those who remain realistic
in their expectations:

> In the first place, screenwriting is *not* hard work, intellectually or physi-
> cally. It is a form of piece work, generally done in collaboration with other
> people, so that even the labor of conception is shared. . . . The screenplay
> is only secondarily a *written* thing; it is an elaborate notation, or, put
> another way, a kind of codified visualization. It is the kind of work that does
> not require the writer to wrestle overmuch with the psyche. It can be
> written quickly and, fortunately, rewritten quickly, as the director, in
> wrestling with *his* psyche, discovers that he needs the visualization
> refined.[31]

McMurtry assures his reader that his essay is not written to deni-
grate the craft of screenwriting but to dispel the myth of the suffering artist.

In "Finding the Film," McMurtry discusses another function of
the screenwriter in the movie industry: the role the writer plays in
the selection of films to be produced. The problem of selection is
always formidable for producers and directors, for they are inevitably deluged with more material than they can possibly utilize:
"books, scripts, treatments, scenarios, step-sheets, outlines and
ubiquitous and free-floating 'ideas' surround them like clouds of
gnats." But neither producer nor director can make initial decisions
in the selection of film material; the producer does not have the
talent, and the director does not have the time. The services of a
writer are usually required at this point, and he is given a book to
adapt and a contract. The writer must "find the picture latent in the
book—if there is a picture—or . . . create one if there isn't."[32] The
writer's task also includes a determination of whether the director

will want to do the picture; thus, he must simultaneously evaluate the book in question and the personality of the director and decide whether the two are compatible.

In the last essay in his series on screenwriting, "Properties, Projects, Possibilities," McMurtry argues that a good film can grow only from good material, and he demonstrates that there is myriad material available, most of which can be acquired and produced cheaply.[33] He ends his essay with a long list of material, divided into categories with the logic for their selection, from which excellent movies can be drawn.

McMurtry's eight-essay series is an important addition to the literature of film. It is also valuable in its insight into a craft that is destined to become another facet of literary art in a world increasingly attracted to the visual media. McMurtry himself obviously intends to continue to combine his talents as novelist, filmwriter, and film critic. He has been a contributing editor to the monthly publication of the American Film Institute,[34] *American Film*, since its inception, continues to be active in screenwriting projects,[35] and has projected a book-length study of the cinematic art.

CHAPTER 6

McMurtry's Contribution to Contemporary Literature

I Satire and Black Humor

McMURTRY is unique among Southwestern regionalists in his use of satire and black humor in a context in which these elements have been traditionally absent—the Western novel. The mordant wit that characterizes many of his essays is intensified in his fiction, which often becomes Hogarthian in the savagery of its satire. His cynical view of marriage reaches its height in *All My Friends Are Going To Be Strangers;* the caustic portraits of Uncle Laredo and his wife, Martha, who are so antagonistic toward each other that they live on separate ranches is a monstrously magnified depiction of marital incompatibility. He caricatures sex-crazed Mexicans in the same novel, Petey Ximenes and Antonio (though perhaps these characterizations illustrate a regional ethnic bias against the non-Anglo). His personal antipathy toward the hypocrisy and tawdry icons of the small town is personified in *The Last Picture Show*, particularly in the figures of Herman Popper and Jacy Farrow. McMurtry has said that the small town derives its concept of masculinity and femininity from the examples of the football coach and the high school beauty queen,[1] but the characterizations of Coach Popper and Jacy Farrow undermine these accepted norms for sexual identification.

In "Eros in Archer City," McMurtry wrote that "most of my smalltown contemporaries spent their high-school years trying desperately to be good athletes, because the attitude of the adults had them quite convinced that their sexual identity depended upon their athletic performance."[2] In *The Last Picture Show*, the athletic activities of the boys are supervised by Coach Popper, who certainly

102

offers no model of masculinity for the boys to emulate. Popper's hairy-chested male chauvinism is merely a facade to mask his latent homosexuality. Similarly, Jacy Farrow's cheerleader and beauty queen femininity is exposed for what it really is: narcissistic, callow, meretricious. Jacy's impassioned embraces and kisses with Duane are inevitably theatrical and exhibitionistic; she seeks peer group status through sexual sophistication, and she even stages a temporary marriage with Sonny for the sensationalism and drama it will afford. Even Jacy's mother notes the symptoms of her narcissism: "Who you love is your own pretty self and *what* you really love is knowing you're pretty" (p. 46). It is appropriate that this small-town sex siren is ultimately seduced by the local stud and pool shark, Abilene, who treats her as if she were a depersonalized sex object—something to be played with between pool shots.

Jacy, the symbol of Thalia's femininity, is seduced in the local male bastion, the pool hall. Abilene takes her there after it has closed for the night to demonstrate his proficiency in shooting pool. Jacy is fascinated by Abilene's special cue stick, which has obvious phallic significance. He handles it "as lovingly as if it were a part of his body," "now lifting the cue and dropping it, withdrawing it and shoving it forward, drawing out every stroke." His game of pool continues the sexual symbolism: "He put the white cue ball in the center of the table, sighted quickly, and then with a quick hard thrust of his hips sent the white ball ramming into the tight triangle of red balls. There was a sharp crack, and the red balls scattered and rolled all over the table" (pp. 217–218). Abilene actually seduces Jacy via his pool playing: "Abilene was totally absorbed in the table full of balls, and Jacy became almost as absorbed in the lovely movements of the cue." When the seduction occurs (atop the pool table), he plays the game of sex the way he plays pool—*cool*: "He was just going on, absorbed in himself, moving, nudging, thrusting—she was no more than an object." Jacy's climax is the final act of the game: "He played her out as recklessly as he had played the final ball, and when he did she scattered as the red balls had scattered when the white one struck them so hard" (pp. 218–221).

The scene of Jacy's ironic seduction by Abilene is full of the caustic humor so characteristic of the novel. Humor was noticeably absent in *Horseman, Pass By*, and although there is considerable humor of the traditional joshing, Southwest variety in *Leaving*

Cheyenne (particularly in the conversations between Johnny and Gid in Johnny's section of the novel), *The Last Picture Show* represents McMurtry's only extensive use of a contemporary development in American humor, black humor.[3] This humor is often reflected in the names of his characters. Sonny's girl, who allows him to fondle her breasts but to do no more, is named Charlene Duggs, and Sonny drives a gas truck for Frank Fartley, who operates a compressed gas company. Black humor is more apparent in McMurtry's descriptions of adolescent sexual activity. Charlene Duggs "kissed convulsively, as if she had just swallowed a golf ball and was trying to force it back up" (p. 13). When Sonny ceases to be satisfied with just fondling Charlene's breast ("it might have been an apple someone had given him just when he was least hungry"), she refuses to let him go further: "you ain't good lookin' enough," she says coldly. "You ain't even got a ducktail. Why should I let you fiddle around and get me pregnant?" (pp. 22–23).

In McMurtry's reference to the practice of bestiality among the country boys, the same type of humor creeps in:

Many of the town kids were also versatile and resourceful—the only difficulty was that they had access to a smaller and less varied animal population. Even so, one spindly sophomore whose father sold insurance had once been surprised in ecstatic union with a roan cocker spaniel, and a degraded youth from the north side of town got so desperate one day that he crawled into a neighbor's pig pen in broad daylight and did it with a sow. [p. 103]

The whole incident of the boys' copulating with the blind heifer is full of the same vein of humor, as is the subsequent coupling of the idiot Billy with the carhop-whore, Jimmie Sue. These two incidents are also very significant to the central theme of the book: the loss of innocence and the subsequent maturation of the protagonist, Sonny Crawford.

Jimmie Sue, the carhop-harlot, affords another example of McMurtry's use of black humor. In her one adventure outside the environs of Thalia, she rode a bus to California seeking excitement and employment, but she had to hitchhike back to Thalia after her suitcase was stolen in the Los Angeles bus station. En route she was picked up by a "carful of horny Mexicans," and later by a Negro. "By the time she got back to Thalia she had nothing good to say about minority groups" (pp. 107–108).

Masturbation is prevalent among the young adolescents, and McMurtry is again a black humorist in his description of Joe Bob Blanton, the Methodist preacher's son, who continues the practice even after his father told him the old bugaboo about masturbation's causing insanity: "He kept right on playing with himself, all through high school, in the face of certain insanity. His father hadn't told him how long it took for a mind to be destroyed, but he never doubted that his would be, sooner or later. . . . he had decided to resign himself to eventual insanity, and he ceased to make any effort to curb his self-abuse" (pp. 208–209). Even the account of Joe Bob's "sexual molestation" of a little girl and the subsequent actions of his hypocritical preacher father are in the tradition of the black humorist.

There is much of this type of humor in Duane's anticlimactic "seduction" of Jacy, as there is in her actual seduction by Abilene. In the first incident, Jacy "sucked in her breath, preparing to be painfully devirginized" (she isn't, and is bitterly disappointed), and in Abilene's poolroom seduction she lies cruciform atop the pool table in eagerly expectant martyrdom: "She stretched her arms above her head and caught her fingers in the corner pockets, sucking in her breath" (p. 219).

McMurtry's use of black humor in *The Last Picture Show* should not be overemphasized, for the novel is a highly symbolic and complex work, as well as a scathing denunciation of the spiritual stagnation of a small town. But it should be noted that the frank treatment of sex in this novel sets it apart from the stereotypes established in such typically Western books as Owen Wister's *The Virginian*, while the humorous treatment of the same subject exhibits the approach utilized by other young Texas writers, such as Donald Barthelme and Terry Southern, or by James Leo Herlihy in *Midnight Cowboy*.[4]

II Use of Mythic, Regional, and Autobiographical Material

When McMurtry published his first novel at the age of twenty-four, both A. B. Guthrie, Jr., and John Howard Griffin praised his realistic handling of Western material. Griffin wrote, "I spent a good deal of time in the ranching country he describes, and this is probably the starkest, most truthful, most terrible and yet beautiful treatment of it I've seen. It will offend many, who prefer the glamour treatment—but it is a true portrait of the loneliness and pervading melancholy of cowboying; and of its compensations in nature, in human relationships."[5] McMurtry often uses the legends of the old West in his fiction, including the stories he heard as a boy at the McMurtry family reunions. One of these stories concerns the rancher Charles Goodnight and the band of ragged Comanches who rode from their reservation in Oklahoma to beg a buffalo from him. At first, the old rancher refused, thinking the Indians would merely drive the buffalo back to their reservation to slaughter and eat it. When he finally consented, the Indians, "whipping up their thin, miserable ponies," ran the buffalo before him and killed it with lances and arrows in a final, ritualistic hunt. Afterward, they "sat looking at it for a time, remembering glories and centuries gone."[6] The story of the last hunt of the Indians is retold by McMurtry in *In a Narrow Grave* and is incorporated in the narrative of *All My Friends Are Going To Be Strangers*. McMurtry also utilizes the legendary exploits of his own family in his fiction. His eccentric Uncle Johnny, for example, described at great length in *In a Narrow Grave*, is obviously the model for Danny Deck's Uncle Laredo in *All My Friends Are Going To Be Strangers*.

Although McMurtry tends to minimize the autobiographical aspects of his fiction, it is quite apparent that many of the characters, particularly in the urban trilogy, are based on his own personality and experience. He has admitted that there is "some element of emotional autobiography in almost any novel," but, he insists, "the things that happen in my books happen to the people in them, the imagined characters I have created."[7] McMurtry later commented further on the autobiographical element in his works: "I may cover this element over so deeply," he says, "that I can't recognize myself (I once let a psychiatrist read my two novels and he pointed out in them some things relevant to me as a person to which I had been completely oblivious). But the autobiography is only one layer, or one element, and perhaps a minor one." More important than the element of "emotional autobiography" is the regional character of his work. "The books are about a place, a very particular region," he says, "and the place goes a long way toward determining the books' tone. I think there is a closer connection between prose and geography than has always been noticed—I cannot imagine, for example, writing about West Texas in the lush prose of the deep South. West Texas needs a barer, more stringent prose, and to describe it lushly would constitute a serious incongruity." He reiterates, however, that his fictional characters exist as individuals: "while the books are partly about me, partly about a place, partly about our time, they are, I hope, chiefly about the characters who live them."[8]

III   *Move Toward Sociological Analysis*

If McMurtry's earlier fiction, particularly *Horseman, Pass By* and *Leaving Cheyenne*, leaves more memorable impressions upon the reader than the later urban trilogy, it is because as McMurtry leaves the ranch country of his youth (both literally in his life and as the subject matter for his fiction) his writing becomes more analytical and sociological. McMurtry's love of the land and his admiration for the people who so strongly identify with it combine with his sense of the passing of the old traditions to produce strong characters of almost mythic stature: patriarchs of the plains such as Homer Bannon and Sam the Lion, unbridled free spirits such as Molly, and sympathetic earth mothers such as Halmea and Genevieve. When he removes his characters from the country to the city, they become rootless seekers with no real identities; as realistic postwar urbanites, they are ultimately less sympathetic than the people in his earlier novels.

McMurtry's departure from the country as subject matter for his fiction begins with *The Last Picture Show*, a book that apparently reflects his own disenchantment with the small town. In a letter to his friend Mike Kunkel, written in Houston on December 3, 1955, McMurtry states his dissatisfaction with the people at Rice University ("a vastly overrated aggregation of uppermiddle class snobs and first rate psychopaths") and his nostalgia for Archer City: "You were right. I did hate to leave. And always will. I am more and more fascinated by the town. Don't know what I'd do if it weren't for it to go home to and dream about." The next month, however, he wrote to Kunkel, "Archer City is rather a mess. If I didn't love the place I'd hate it violently. A bunch of almost inextricably mixed up kids," and on August 31, 1956, he wrote Kunkel from Archer City: "You can't imagine how horrible it is to be the least bit different from your provincial fellow man. . . . This is the damndest town for petty feuds I ever saw—almost everybody hates almost everybody else."

The Last Picture Show also exhibits a sociological emphasis absent in McMurtry's earlier novels. This approach is continued in his urban novels, particularly in their examination of modern marriage and the displacement of the cowboy to an urban environment. Although *The Last Picture Show* gained much notoriety for its many explicit sexual scenes, McMurtry has treated sex frankly in his fiction from the beginning. The editorial correspondence concerning *Horseman, Pass by*, reveals that the book contained much more sexual vocabulary than appeared in the published version; the text was altered considerably at the suggestion of McMurtry's editor to preserve the innocence of the young narrator, Lonnie.[10] McMurtry's emphasis on sex is yet another aspect of his fiction that distinguishes it from the work of other western writers.

A further indication of McMurtry's interest in social criticism is his most recent nonfiction, where he moves from consideration of Southwestern themes to subjects of topical and national concern, such as the sexual revolution and the Watergate scandals. McMurtry has always been an able satirist; his early spoofing of Texas and Texans in *Holiday* magazine and in the *Texas Observer* are examples. In his most recent nonfiction, he applies his trenchant wit in the perceptive analysis of issues affecting contemporary American culture.

When the entire nation was following each televised episode of the painfully drawn out Watergate conspiracy trials as avidly as they would a serialized soap opera, and when the public snapped up the first installment of the lengthy (if expurgated) transcripts of the taped conversations of President Nixon and his codefendants in the hearings, McMurtry, in an essay entitled "Best Seller! A Novelist Looks at 'Verbal Evil' and the Presidential Transcripts as Bedside Reading," "reviewed" the text as if it were a national best-seller.[11] McMurtry says that he wanted to understand and, if possible, participate in the widespread moral indignation that had caused him to "sit down and slog through the whole 1,308-page record." He had hoped that reading the massive documentary "just this once" would cause him to become "as disillusioned and morally indignant" as the rest of America, but when he finished reading that book, he found that his "moral pulse" was beating no faster; instead, he was "more intrigued by the outcry than by the men or the events that caused it." His reaction might have prompted him to preface his essay with a quotation from Edward Gibbon: "The most worthless of mankind are not afraid to condemn in others the same disorders which they allow themselves; and can readily discover some nice difference of age, character, or station, to justify the partial distinction." McMurtry seems to feel that the chronicle of corruption revealed in the taped conversations symptomized a national malaise:

Americans, it would seem, demand a facade of virtue from their Presidents which is possibly as incompatible with the practice of high politics as it would be with with the practice of high art. In recent decades Presidential virtue, or, or least, Presidential probity has become the lonely pillar that supports the myth of our national innocence, and for Americans to have to think of themselves as other than innocent is an excruciating moral ordeal. President Nixon, through his unremitting, compulsive practice of the craft that raised him so high, has now inadvertently forced this ordeal upon us. He cracked the facade, broke the pillar, and brought the myth tumbling down in our laps; our innocence is tarnished forever, or at least until 1976 (p. 27).

McMurtry predicted that the President would resign a few months later. "What is underway now," he wrote, "is a purification rite straight out of *The Golden Bough*. Our temporary king has accidentally drawn to himself the national guilt—over race, over Vietnam, over how many decades of casual public corruption and private turpitude?—and the ritual won't stop until his heart has been cut out and laid on Plymouth Rock, so that the crop of our innocence will grow again."[12] He did not, however, feel that Nixon and his confederates in the Watergate conspiracy should be exonerated—far from it—but instead of responding to them with a moral outrage and indignation, he looked at them with the cold eye of a satirist, portraying them now as dull, unimaginative characters in an absurdist drama, now as stereotypes from a B-grade movie.

In his "book review," McMurtry treated the transcripts as a rather boring literary work. He called the "book" particularly weak in its dialogue and singled out Nixon's inelegance of language for attack. "I can see how a President might have difficulties being honest, in these times, but there is really no excuse for such ineloquence. After all, a great many of our Presidents have been, like Mr. Nixon, practiced hypocrites; how can we tell the great man from the small except insofar as they put things well?" If Jefferson and Lincoln were not always noble men, McMurtry reminded, they were always capable of noble prose when occasion demanded it:

Alas—looking to Mr. Nixon for eloquence is like looking to Arizona for truffles. Reading the transcripts straight through induces in one a state of emotional numbness such as might occur if one were for some reason compelled to sit down and read the collected works of Samuel Beckett seven or eight times in the course of a week. It is as if "Waiting for Godot," "Krapp's Last Tape," and "Endgame" had been crudely spliced together; as drama its only virtue is that it could be simply staged—perhaps one could use giant

Oval Room Wastebaskets instead of ashcans. The small cast, the limited vocabulary, the over-riding repetitiveness and monotony of the dialogue, the passivity, the mental immobility, the sense that even one's doom is going to turn out to be dull—all these are suggestive of Beckett.[13]

It is obvious, said McMurtry, that "the four principals—President Nixon, Mr. Haldeman, Mr. Erlichman, and Mr. Dean"—had a "persistent sense of themselves as being characters in a drama. The terminology of the screen, or, at least, the television studio, is omnipresent in the dialogue." In commenting on the "dialogue," McMurtry observed that the language of the transcript generally derived from Hemingway, "but it is Hemingway filtered through his pulp-magazine imitators into B-movie dialogue," which, McMurtry suggested, is probably where the four learned it. "Usages derived from old private-eye movies are pervasive. 'Heat' is to be put on the Speaker of the House, Magruder is apt to 'finger' various people, some of whom will be required to 'take a dive.' "[14]

"Best Seller!" is McMurtry's first extended commentary on political issues; with the exception of a 1968 letter to the editor of the *Houston Post*, his earlier essays were generally confined to Southwestern subjects or to film criticism.[15] His recent essays, however, have followed the social analysis that characterizes his urban trilogy. One essay, "Your Place or Mine: Speculations on Female Macho," elucidates some of the themes and characterizations of these novels. In "Your Place or Mine" McMurtry examines the women's movement, the sexual revolution, and the new permissiveness in discussions of sex. McMurtry has always had a penchant for strong women, but women who are strong and feminine at the same time (examples are the women in his first three novels); he is concerned about a newly emergent woman who exhibits what he calls female macho. The concept of female macho, says McMurtry, "is a convenient way of high-lighting in the behavior of women a kind of romantic bravura that fewer and fewer men can feel comfortable in claiming for themselves." McMurtry recommends a reading of Octavio Paz's *The Labyrinth of Solitude* for the true meaning of macho. Paz sees the macho as one who has no inner peace, one who is condemned by his own attitudes and instincts to a perpetual and anxious solitude, who sees all social intercourse as combat, and whose "pride is desperate, his touchiness extreme, his security nil." McMurtry's paraphrase of Paz brings to mind Sonny Shanks in *Mov-*

ing On. In stealing the term *macho* from the Spanish, says McMurtry, American have romanticized it: "We do not think of someone with machismo as lonely, anxious, or unable to communicate; we merely think of such a person as tough and in control. Yet all that a *macho* can possibly be in control of is his own isolation, and even that control is sure to be constantly threatened." Actually, "machismo is essentially fascistic, in men or women; its allegiance is to power, rather than intelligence, to force rather than feeling."[16]

Referring to the prevalence of the syndrome among university students, McMurtry says that "central to the whole issue on campus, it would seem, is the question of separateness, and of rejection. 'Our place' is heard less and less often; nowadays it's your place or mine, and boys and girls alike talk of sexual rejection with the seriousness with which middle-aged people talk of terminal cancer."[17]

In discussing the new permissiveness in sexual discussions, McMurtry says that "all the frank talk that has come with the well-publicized sexual revolution of the 1960s has on the whole been less stimulating, less informative, less creative, and duller than the repressed and nuance-ridden talk of the decades which preceded it; the populist sex-is-perfectly-normal-everybody-talk-about-it approach, with its free if de-energized use of four-letter words, offers just as rigid a verbal convention as any other, and moreover it conceals at its heart the fanciful belief rather trustingly taken over from psychotherapy that sexual anxieties diminish in proportion to how freely they can be talked about."[18]

Jenny Salomea in *All My Friends Are Going To Be Strangers* illustrates McMurtry's theory. She first enters the narrative of the novel asking the protagonist if his wife likes cunnilingus and coaxing him to have oral sex with her. When she fails in her attempts, she plays a desperate game of machismo with him: "If you don't think you know how say so and I'll go home and get drunk. You're not as *macho* about sex as you are about badminton, are you?" (p. 20). But despite her explicit vocabulary and her aggressive manner, Jenny is lonely, desperate, and sexually inexperienced. When Danny finally has sex with her, he notes that "she was a long way from knowing how to really enjoy herself. . . . She just hadn't had any practice" (p. 216). Danny asks her about the inconsistency between her image as "Jenny Salomea, the man-eater" and the true facts: " 'You're supposed to be very tough,' I said. 'I am tough,' she said. 'That's why I never sleep with anybody. I'm so tough men are afraid to try me. It just makes me worse. If I can scare them I don't want to do it with them anyway' " (p. 215). Jenny has hidden her inhibitions, frustrations, and anxious loneliness behind a facade of frank speech and machismo, but as McMurtry notes in his essay, "only those folks who are simpleheaded enough to believe that organic gardening can do the job truth has never been able to do, i.e., make us free and healthy, could suppose that uninhibited sexual commentary has finally done in the old hydra of sexual anxiety. A glance down any street should dispel that notion."[19]

IV Characterization and Dialogue

McMurtry's urban Westerns represent his greatest contribution to contemporary Western literature. It is yet too early to trace his influence on other regionalists of his generation; but even now it is evident that he is the leader, if not the sole practitioner, in the development of the modern Western novel. John Rechy, in a series of novels beginning with his *City of Night,* also writes of dispossessed Texans in an urban environment. His protagonists, however— Johnny Rio, Chuck, Jim—are inevitably mere avatars of the cowboy cum street hustler that personifies the limited homosexual perspective of all his novels. In contrast, McMurtry's urban Westerns embrace an entire society, not just the underworld of the gay community; his novels are peopled with the very rich (Vernon Dalhart, Eleanor Guthrie), the middle class (Jim Carpenter, Flap Horton), the lower middle class (Hank Malory, Sally Bynum), and the lower class (Pee Wee Baskin, Royce Dunlap). His themes are universal, for whether it be loneliness, frustration, infidelity, or the dissolution of marriage, the condition is omnipresent among all the classes of society.

McMurtry's classes are clearly differentiated through his skillful use of characterization and dialogue. The cowboys of the earlier novels have become rodeo performers in his urban settings; his rural ranch hands have become "city billies" performing menial tasks in the back streets of the metropolis. Yet both retain the vestigial remnants of their roots—as if a bit of the rural sod still clings to the cuffs of their rhinestone rodeo suits or the hubcaps of their pickup trucks. McMurtry achieves this effect through his characterization; whether he is describing bored graduate students or drunken potato chip truck drivers, the actions of his characters are always appropriate to the type being delineated.

The social classes are further differentiated by their speech: the wealthy are suitably sophisticated and cynical in their pronouncements,[20] the graduate students are self-consciously jaded and literate in their conversations, and the housewives are characteristically whining and self-pitying in their exchange of confidences. McMurtry is most adroit in his creation of lower-class dialogue, capturing the twang of the west Texan, the gift of metaphor and simile of the east Texan, the frustration and ill-contained rage of the redneck, the nuances of defeat in the speech of the working class. His gift for constructing convincing dialogue is not restricted to the regionalisms of his Texas types, as he demonstrates in the sparkling repartee of the wealthy Boston widow, Aurora Greenway, in *Terms of Endearment.*

V   Conclusion

McMurtry's tendency to become more sociological in his recent fiction is concomitant with a move away from the symbolism present in his earlier works. In a letter of August 27, 1957, McMurtry wrote to his friend Mike Kunkel concerning his attraction to symbolic writing: "I was once leery of symbolism, but it has become such a standard tool that now I am equally leery of absence of same, like some people shy from the absence of rhyme and meter in poetry." The beautifully handled symbolism of his earlier fiction, however—such as the slaughter of the herd, the longhorn steers, the wail of passing trains across the prairie—is absent in the novels written in an urban context. The contrast between his later style and his earlier work is illustrated in the comparison of how he evokes the feeling of loneliness in his characters. In his first novel, *Horseman, Pass By*, McMurtry devotes three pages of the prologue to creating the mood of loneliness that overpowers the young narrator. Bull bats swoop low over the lilac bushes in the fading light, horses clop past the yard on their way to the dark grazing grounds below the hill, the big diesel trucks growl down the highway a mile distant across the prairie, the calves in the passing cattle train bawl their "lonesome sound at twilight," and whippoorwills, "the ghostly birds" that Lonnie never sees, call across the flats below the ridge. In *The Last Picture Show*, the images of loneliness are confined to one page. Sonny feels "like he is the only human creature in the town" because of "the look of the town": a single car is parked on the courthouse square, a cold norther sings off the plains and swirls long ribbons of dust down empty Main Street, and no one is coming down the highway that leads into town (p. 1). In his fourth novel, *Moving On*, loneliness is expressed without symbolism or imagery: "Patsy had never thought of herself as a lonely person and had never believed that loneliness would be a problem—not for her. . . . She had read a lot about loneliness and knew it was one of the great problems of modern life, but it had never been very real to her" (p. 393).

The future course of McMurtry's fiction would seem to be in the direction of further sociological analysis of modern urban life written in the stark style of *Moving On* and *All My Friends Are Going To Be Strangers*. McMurtry has never returned to the subject of the land and the people who live on it, and he has indicated that he does not intend to use Texas materials in any presently projected novels, but that he might use his experience in California as the subject for future works.[21] His determination not to use the regional material of his earlier work indicates that he will move toward more topical and nonregional themes in the future. Even his urban trilogy has, in the process of creation, grown away from the regionalism that characterized his earlier works. McMurtry has become even more alienated from his region since his move to Washington. In an essay published in 1975 McMurtry writes that he considers himself a "happily exiled native son who no longer feels very native or anything like a son" and who, after a return to his home state for a few weeks," comes away wondering vaguely why it was he lived there so long."[22] Exile, he says, gives one perspective, and he apparently feels that he has written all he can about Texas and must move on to more fertile fields for his imagination:

Writers—novelists, at least—tend to be imperialists in their use of place. They exploit a given region, suck what thematic riches they can from it, and then, if they are able, move on to whatever regions promise yet more riches. I was halfway through my sixth Texas novel when I suddenly began to notice that where place was concerned, I was sucking air. The book is set in Houston, but none of the characters are Texans. Somehow, without attending to what I was doing, I had assembled an international cast, one that included a broken-down opera singer from Genoa, a playboy from Philadelphia, a retired general from Connecticut, and, first and foremost, a widow from Boston, Massachusetts. At first this development shocked me, but now that I've had time to think about it, I think it's probably for the best. My imagination has been peopled exclusively by Texans for long enough. A given place, after all, will produce a finite number of local styles, and a finite number of mental sets. A new place, such as Texas, will have developed fewer styles, less complex manners, and less intricate patterns of mental and emotional behavior than an old place, like Boston. The novel feeds on manners, styles, and intricate social expressions, which is why American writers from the West and Midwest have traditionally tended to graze eastward. A region is inexhaustible fictionally only if one finds in its history a profound and tragic resonance—what Faulkner found in the guilty, slave-ridden South.[23]

Texas, says McMurtry, does not have the "tragic resonance" of Faulkner's country; its history is a history of land wars—"common to mankind as dirt, and which have no prevailing guilt." When McMurtry is asked why he, a "true-born Texan," moved East, he replies that he had grown tired of dealing creatively with the "mental and emotive inarticulateness" that he found in Texas. "The move off the land is now virtually completed, and that was the great subject that Texas offered writers of my generation. The one basic subject it offers us now is loneliness, and one can ring changes on that so many times."[24] McMurtry himself has been part of the move away from the land, a land he loved, spent thirty-two years on, and wrote six books about before abandoning it for the East. And in this essay, written five years after his departure, there is still the old ambivalence and the loneliness beneath his pronouncements that he does not wish to return to his native state: *"You Can't Go Home Again* seems to me to be an unconsciously misleading title—its silent assumption is that everyone wants to, when in fact a great many people would rather not, at least not to live."[25] McMurtry would prefer not to return home because it has become something he does not like. Perhaps it was never anything he liked; perhaps what held him in thrall was the myth of the West, a myth about which he has always had the most ambivalent of feelings. He struggled to separate the reality of his region from its mythology in the collection of essays published in 1968, and in 1975, after five years of self-imposed expatriation, he began an essay on Texas with a statement that reveals he is still not free of the myth, his protestations to the contrary.

In the years that I have been writing about Texas, I have always found that my initial, and my hardest, task has been to convince myself that the Texas I have lived in and in some sense known was as legitimate and as worthy of attention as the Texas that existed before my time. All through my youth I listened to stories about an earlier, purer, a more golden and more legendary Texas that I had been born too late to see.[26]

The romance of these myths underpins much of McMurtry's most successful fiction; his struggle to free himself from it forms the conflict present in the best of his nonfiction. But contemporary Texas has become a place where not only the legendary figures of the old myths have disappeared, but where even the myths themselves are fast vanishing. "Oilmen," says McMurtry, "seem to be the only people who can afford the cattle business, mythologically or otherwise. Elsewhere, the romance and the imagery of the range have faded—off the land, off the movie screens, out of the books; even, for the most part, out of country music; and when a myth fades out of country music, it cannot be holding much of a place in the public minds." McMurtry writes that throughout this century, two figures have stood in polarity in the mythology of the region: the cowboy and the millionaire oilman. The cowboy is gone; "Texas belongs to the oilmen now, and they know it. Money—Big Money—provides the only mythology presently active in Texas."[27] It is a new mythology, one with which McMurtry cannot identify: "Wealth, the wealthy, and the accoutrements of wealth are the commonest source of anecdote and legend in Houston and Dallas, or Austin and Amarillo, or San Antonio and Lubbock. Husbandry still exists, as do herdspeople, but the enterprise is secondary economically, and the people who continue to practice it are diehards, sociologically retrograde."[28]

Homer Bannon represents such a "diehard" in the struggle against economic modernity in his state; his reaction to the veterinarian's suggestion to lease his grazing land to the oil companies is representative of the type. The old man does not want oil wells because he can not ride among them, breed them, or rope them as he can his herd. Most importantly, he does not want oil money; he wants his money to come from "something that keeps a man doing for himself." The old rancher's killing of the two longhorn steers, cattle that he had raised to remind him of "how times were," signals not only the death of the old man himself but the passing of an era. Hud, of course, is not averse to leasing the lands to an oil company for fast profit, nor is he sentimental about ranching.

In Faulkner's epic saga of the South, a new breed of man, the Snopeses, arises after the Civil War to challenge not only the power but the life-styles and values of the old aristocracy. The emergence of this class signals the birth of the new South and the end of the old mythic South. Faulkner was able to chronicle the demise of the old traditions and to reconstruct the antebellum South in his art while avoiding the pitfalls of historical romance. He succeeds, ultimately, in utilizing the materials of mythology to restore the old South in a kind of living presence, one in which he was totally at home. For more than a decade, McMurtry's task has been not so much to restore the myth of the West as to lay it to rest, to escape from its hold. Indeed, McMurtry has never been fully convinced of the accuracy of the myth, but whether he conceives of it as something that was, or that might have or should have been, his conception of the old West as myth gave form to his earliest fiction and ennobles some of his most memorable characters: Homer Bannon, Sam the Lion, and Roger Waggoner.

If McMurtry is ambiguous about what the myth was, he is convinced that it is now irretrievably lost, and this conviction causes the tension in his art. In 1968, in his introduction to *In a Narrow Grave,* McMurtry wrote that living in his region involved him at once in "a birth, a death, and a bitter love affair" (p. xv). From the birth, he says he expects very little, for the "new Texas is probably going to be a sort of kid brother to California, with a kid brother's tendency to imitation."[29] The death, however, moved him, for "the way of life that is dying had its value. Its appeal was simple, but genuine, and it called to it and is taking with it people whom one could not but love." In commenting on his "bitter love affair" with his region, McMurtry says that he should perhaps not call it a *bitter* love affair—"merely one that has become a little too raw, too real, too stripped of fantasy. The time may have come to part or marry, but, for myself, I put no trust in either alternative. Parting would not leave me free nor marriage make me happy" (p. xvi).

These lines are prophetic. In 1975, McMurtry returned after five years to attempt an objective evaluation of his state for a special Texas issue of the *Atlantic Monthly.*[30] He is critical of what has happened to the state. The oil rich, the unimaginative architecture, the suburbanization of the backlands, the intellectual sterility of the universities—all fall under the cold and analytical eye of the erstwhile native son now become Eastern *auslander.* But when McMurtry examines the area of the state that has changed little since he left it, the wind-swept area about which he had written so

often, he consciously allows his essay to drift toward "the dream."
Caught at night in a raging sandstorm in Roberts County, one of the
bleakest and most sparsely inhabited of the Texas counties, McMurtry enters a café and finds its sole occupant is a waitress he had
known years before in another town. She explains that Roberts
County "was always home," and when her husband died, she moved
back. "Home's home," says. "It's a right friendly place, too." The
drumming of the sand against the window glass seems to soothe the
woman, and she asks McMurtry, "Where do you live at now?"
When McMurtry tells her, she exclaims, "Lord, how do you stand
it, honey? At least this here's in Texas. Don't you get lonesome?"
"Well, I read a lot," he responds.[31] McMurtry's essay closes on this
implicit expression of loneliness and ambivalent feeling toward his
state. Apparently the ghosts of his Uncle Johnny, Charlie Goodnight, and Teddy Blue still haunt McMurtry, though he now lives in
Washington, D.C., far from "his blood's country and his heart's
pastureland."

McMurtry laments that although Texas has "a few decent writers," it has had no Homer and no Faulkner. "Thus," he says, "it has
no single, greatly told tragic story, no central myth." McMurtry
remains preeminently a regional novelist, the finest Texas has yet
produced. Should he overcome the unresolved tension he feels
about his native soil, he might succeed in writing the saga the region
lacks.

Notes and References

Chapter One

1. "An Interview with Larry McMurtry," *Collage* (May 1967).
2. Thomas Landess, *Larry McMurtry* (Austin, 1969).
3. Interview with McMurtry, Oct. 1972, Washington, D.C.
4. Ibid.
5. Ibid.
6. "An Interview with Larry McMurtry," *Collage* (May 1967), p. 7.
7. Ibid.
8. Interview, Oct. 1972.
9. Interview with McMurtry, June 1967, Houston, Texas.
10. Interview, Oct. 1972.
11. Ibid.
12. "An Interview with Larry McMurtry," *Collage* (May 1967).
13. *Collage.*
14. McMurtry, "Dallas: A Reflection," *Gentleman's Quarterly* (March 1966), pp. 128–129, 153.
15. McMurtry, "Texas: Good Times Gone, or Here Again?" *Holiday* (Sept. 1965), pp. 58 ff.

Chapter Two

1. Thomas Landess, *Larry McMurtry* (Austin, 1969), p.6.
2. Ibid, p. 6.
3. "Approaching Cheyenne . . . Leaving Lumet, Oh Pshaw!" *New York*, 7, No. 17 (29 April 1974), 66.
4. Landess, p. 28.
5. Arnold Rosenfeld, "Books: Larry," *Houston Post*, 30 Oct. 1966.
6. Interview with McMurtry, Oct. 1972, Washington, D.C.
7. Ibid.
8. This correspondence is in the Special Collections section of the University of Houston Library.

9. McMurtry, "The Questions a Writer Gets Asked" (speech), Special Collections, University of Houston Library. This is a short version of the speech.

10. The editorial correspondence from John Leggett, McMurtry's editor at Harper's, is in Special Collections, University of Houston Library. Harper's did not publish *Moving On;* Simon and Schuster did.

11. McMurtry, "Questions a Writer Gets Asked" (long version), pp. 15–16. The typescript of the long version is also in Special Collections, University of Houston Library.

12. Typescripts of both this version and other versions of the novel, entitled *The Country of the Horns*, are in Special Collections, University of Houston Library.

13. Interview with McMurtry, Oct. 1972, Washington, D.C.

14. Ibid.

15. Ibid. Logically, Danny could not have drowned. The book is written in the first person form of the narrative and Danny must therefore be recalling the river incident post facto.

16. McMurtry, "Dunlup Crashes In," *Playboy*, 22 (July 1975), 119, 144–154.

17. Janis P. Stout, "Journeying as a Metaphor for Cultural Loss in the Novels of Larry McMurtry," *Western American Literature*, 11 (Spring 1976), 44.

18. Ibid., 45.

Chapter Three

1. Thomas Landess, *Larry McMurtry* (Austin, 1969), p. 13.

2. Kenneth W. Davis, "The Themes of Initiation in the Works of Larry McMurtry and Tom Mayer," *The Arlington Quarterly*, 2 (Winter 1969–1970), p. 41.

3. Interview with McMurtry, June 1967, Houston, Texas.

4. Ibid.

5. *Book Week*, 23 Oct. 1966, p. 16.

6. Interview with McMurtry.

7. The typescript of two chapters of the uncompleted novel, *Our Revels Now Are Ended*, is in Special Collections, University of Houston Library. A manuscript note by McMurtry indicates that the forty-one page typescript dates from "late 1961–early 1962."

8. A typescript with manuscript corrections of *Lovebreaking* is in Special Collections, University of Houston Library. A note McMurtry wrote indicates that the 574-page typescript is the third draft of the novel and was completed in the spring of 1965. The note also indicates that this version of the novel was "abandoned" and "is now in revision as *The Country of the Horn*."

9. *Take My Saddle from the Wall* is one of the working titles of the collection of essays, *In a Narrow Grave*. Another was *The Cowboy's Lament*.

10. *Memories of the Old Tribe* was the title of the first draft of *Leaving Cheyenne*. The typescript (197 pages) with manuscript corrections is in Special Collections, University of Houston Library.

11. A six-page carbon typescript of this unpublished short story is included in McMurtry's letters to Mike Kunkel, Special Collections, University of Houston Library.

12. Two variant texts of this unpublished speech of McMurtry are in Special Collections, University of Houston Library. The first version, a typescript of twelve pages, bears a notation in pencil by McMurtry: "This speech has been delivered 17 times to date—1968." The second version of the speech is a twenty-page typescript. This quotation is from the first version of "The Questions a Writer Gets Asked," p. 6.

13. Ibid., p. 5.

14. Interview with McMurtry, Oct. 1972, Washington, D.C.

15. A 301-page typescript of *The Water and the Blood, A Melodramatic Novel* is in Special Collections, University of Houston Library. The typescript has manuscript corrections and a note in pencil by McMurtry that indicates the date of completion of this draft of the novel. A revision (or second draft) of 299 pages is also housed in Special Collections; note by McMurtry indicates that this second draft was completed in December, 1964.

I am indebted to Marian Orgain, curator of Special Collections at the University of Houston Library, for pointing out the source for this early working title of the novel. The lines in the hymn are:

> Rock of ages, cleft for me,
> Let me hide myself in Thee;
> Let the water and the blood,
> From thy wounded side which flowed,
> Be of sin the double cure,
> Save from wrath and make me pure.

The hymn and the line with the image of the water and the blood are alluded to in *Horseman, Pass By*, p. 168.

16. A typescript of *The Country of the Horns* is in Special Collections, University of Houston Library. John Leggett, McMurtry's editor at Harper's, to McMurtry, 25 May 1964, indicates that at that time the working title of the novel was *Sometimes the Matador*.

17. "Questions a Writer Gets Asked" (short version), p. 5.

18. Ibid. (long version), p. 3.

19. Ibid. (short version), p. 3.

20. A typescript (197 pages) with manuscript corrections of *Memories of the Old Tribe* is in Special Collections, University of Houston Library. This early draft differs considerably from the published novel.

21. Curiously, the title *Leaving Cheyenne* was originally intended to be used as the title for a nonfiction work; among the unpublished McMurtry material in Special Collections, University of Houston Library, is a three-page outline for a projected book to be entitled *Leaving Cheyenne: Essays on American Rodeo.* The outline indicates that the book was to be "fifty to sixty thousand words; twelve to fourteen chapters of four to five thousand words each." A note in pencil by McMurtry reads, "I drew up the enclosed outline in 1962 and traveled some 7,000 miles before giving up on the book." The outline of the projected book is included in a folder with three pages of manuscript notes by McMurtry concerning the format of the book, illustrations he wishes to use, and riders he wants to interview.

22. The editorial correspondence from Leggett to McMurtry concerning McMurtry's first novels is quite extensive. It is housed in Special Collections, University of Houston Library.

23. "Questions a Writer Gets Asked" (long version), p. 16.

24. Interview, Oct. 1972.

Chapter Four

1. McMurtry, "Answer from McMurtry," *Texas Observer*, 63 (26 Feb. 1971) 22–24.

2. I have treated this function of McMurtry's female characters in my article, "Coming of Age in Texas: The Novels of Larry McMurtry," *Western American Literature*, 4 (Fall 1969), 188.

3. Inez Hernandez Tovar, "The Quest Theme in the Fiction of Larry McMurtry" (Master's thesis, University of Houston, 1972). See particularly chapter 4, "The Mother-Lover Figure as Counselor." A condensed and slightly modified version of her research was presented in a paper, "The Archetype of Woman in the Fiction of Larry McMurtry," at the Fourth National Convention of the Popular Culture Association in Milwaukee, Wisconsin, May 1974.

4. Ibid., p. iv.

5. Jimmie Clifton Sniffen, "The Emergence of Woman in the Novels of Larry McMurtry" (Master's thesis, Stephen F. Austin State University, 1972) abstract.

6. Ibid.

7. Billie Phillips, "McMurtry's Women: *Eros (Libido, Caritas,* and *Philia)* in (and out of) Archer County," paper read at the Fourth Annual Convention of the Popular Culture Association.

8. Rollo May, *Love and Will* (New York: W.W. Norton, 1969), pp. 37–38. Interview with McMurtry, Oct. 1972, Washington, D.C.

9. Interview with McMurtry, Oct. 1972, Washington, D.C.

10. Ibid.

11. Ibid.

12. Ibid.

13. Pauline Kael, "*Hud*, Deep in the Divided Heart of Hollywood," *Film Quarterly*, 17, No. 4 (Summer 1964), 17.

14. "Here's HUD in Your Eye," *In a Narrow Grave*, p. 14.

15. Interview with McMurtry.

16. Ibid.

17. Ibid.

18. "Here's HUD," p. 17.

19. Ibid. pp. 16, 19.

20. McMurtry, "Cowboys, Movies, Myths, and Cadillacs: Realism in the Western," In *Man and the Movies*, ed. W. R. Robinson, (Baton Rouge, 1967), p. 50. A slightly different version of the essay, retitled "Cowboys, Movies, Myths, and Cadillacs: An Excursus on Ritual Forms in the Western Movie," was published in *In a Narrow Grave*.

21. Ibid., pp. 50–51.

22. Ibid., pp. 42, 51, 52.

23. Ibid.

24. Ibid., p. 42.

25. Ibid., McMurtry. "Goat-Ropers and Groupies: A Requiem for a Rodeo," *New York*, 5 (27 Nov. 1972), 58.

26. Ibid. p. 61.

27. Thomas Landess, *Larry McMurtry* (Austin, 1969), p. 33.

28. Interview with McMurtry.

Chapter Five

1. Besides his collaboration with Peter Bogdanovich on the film script for the movie adaptation of *The Last Picture Show*, and a script for an unproduced film about "the end of the West," McMurtry wrote a 357-page screenplay, *Spawn of Evil*. The typescript, which is in Special Collections, University of Houston Library, is dated May–June 1965. In the same collection is "Spawn of Evil–A Synopsis," a typescript of 134 pages dated July 1965. A note in McMurtry's hand indicates that this is a brief treatment of a new story to be included in the original screenplay.

2. "Here's HUD in Your Eye," *In a Narrow Grave*, p. 17.

3. Ibid. The screenplay was written by Irving Ravetch and Harriet Frank, Jr.

4. Interview with McMurtry, Oct. 1972, Washington, D.C.

5. Pauline Kael, "*Hud*, Deep in the Divided Heart of Hollywood," *Film Quarterly*, 17, No. 4 (Summer 1964), 15–16.

6. "Here's HUD in Your Eye," p. 17.

7. Pauline Degenfelder, "McMurtry and the Movies: *Hud* and *The Last Picture Show*," *Western Humanities Review*, 29 (Winter 1975), 84–85.

8. Ibid., p. 85.

9. *In a Narrow Grave*, p. 19.

10. Interview with McMurtry.

11. Ibid. For a full discussion of the plot of the projected movie, see McMurtry, "Personal Factors," *American Film*, 1 (March 1976), 7, 73. It is also mentioned in McMurtry's "Finding the Film," *American Film*, 1 (May 1976), 7, 74.

12. McMurtry, "Movie-Tripping: My Own Rotten Film Festival," *New York*, 6 (5 Feb. 1973), 38.

13. Ibid., 38, 39, 48.

14. "An Interview with Larry McMurtry," *Collage*, May 1967, p. 8.

15. Larry McMurtry, "*The Last Picture Show*: A Last Word," *Colonial Times*, 1, No. 4 (21 Dec.–12 Jan. 1972), 1, 14.

16. Ibid., p. 16.

17. The casting of Ben Johnson in the role of Sam the Lion was fortuitous; Johnson, a veteran of Western films such as *Shane, Rio Grande*, and *The Wild Bunch*, personifies the quiet masculine dignity, honesty, and strength of the cowboy archetype—a vestigial renmant of the old West of the ranges amid the drab town of the new West whose boys define their masculinity through high school athletics, zoophilia, and group sex. In his role, Johnson projects the same patriarchal quality and masculine presence as did Melvyn Douglas in the role of Homer Bannon.

18. "*The Last Picture Show*: A Last Word," p. 14.

19. Ibid.

20. McMurtry, "The Last Word on 'The Last Picture Show,' " *The Daily Rag*, 1 No. 1 (Oct. 1972), 13.

21. McMurtry, "Cowboys, Movies, Myths, and Cadillacs," in *Man and the Movies* (Baton Rouge, 1967), pp. 46–52. The original title of the essay was "Cowboys, Movies, Myths, and Cadillacs: Realism in the Western." It was published in a slightly variant form as "Cowboys, Movies, Myths, and Cadillacs: An Excursus on Ritual Forms in the Western Movie," in *In a Narrow Grave*, pp. 21–29. Larry McMurtry, "Movie-Tripping: My Own Rotten Film Festival," *New York*, 6 No. 6 (5, Feb. 1973), 38–49.

22. "Approaching Cheyenne . . . Leaving Lumet, Oh, Pshaw!" *New York*, 7, No. 17 (29 April 1974), 64–66.

23. Ibid., p. 68.

24. Ibid., p. 66.

25. McMurtry, "Goat-Ropers and Groupies," p. 60.

26. McMurtry, "No Clue, or Learning to Write for the Movies," *American Film*, 1 (October 1975): 9–12.

27. McMurtry, "The Hired Pen," *American Film*, 1 (Nov. 1975), 4–5, 71.

28. McMurtry, "The Deadline Syndrome," *American Film*, 1 (Dec. 1975), 4–5, 69.

29. McMurtry, "The Telephone Book Screenwriter," *American Film*, 1 (Jan.–Feb. 1976), 8–9, 65.

30. McMurtry, "Personal Factors," *American Film*, 1 (Mar. 1976), 6–7, 73.

31. McMurtry, "The Fun of It All," *American Film*, 1 (April 1976), 54–55, 90.

32. McMurtry, "Finding the Film," *American Film*, 1 (May 1976), 6–7, 74.

33. McMurtry, "Properties, Projects, Possibilities," *American Film*, 1 (June 1976), 6–7, 79.

34. The American Film Institute is a nonprofit organization established in 1967 by the National Endowment for the Arts to advance the art of film and television in the United States.

35. For a complete listing of McMurtry's screenwriting activities since his collaboration on the script of *The Last Picture Show*, see "Finding the Film," pp. 7, 74.

Chapter Six

1. "An Interview with Larry McMurtry" *Collage*, May 1967, p. 8.

2. McMurtry "Eros in Archer City," *In a Narrow Grave*, p. 65.

3. Although there is black humor in *All My Friends Are Going To Be Strangers*, as in the scenes on Uncle Laredo's ranch and in the Leon O'Reilly episode in Hollywood. *The Last Picture Show* is characterized by a consistent use of this type of humor.

4. When one remembers the sexual squeamishness of Owen Wister's protoptypic Western, in which the hero, on his honeymoon, sets up two separate and private swimming holes, it is not difficult to see how far McMurtry has carried the genre. Typically, the Western novel has ignored the sexual experience. See David D. Davis's treatment of this subject in "Ten-Gallon Hero," *American Quarterly*, 6 (Summer 1954), 111–125.

5. John Howard Griffin to McMurtry's agent at Harper and Row, March 20, 1961. This portion of the letter was used as the dust jacket blurb; a copy of the complete letter from Griffin is in Special Collections, University of Houston Library.

6. *In a Narrow Grave*, pp. 18–19.

7. McMurtry, "The Questions a Writer Gets Asked" (short version), p. 9, Special Collections, University of Houston Library.

8. Ibid. (long version), pp. 18–20.

9. In Special Collections, University of Houston Library.

10. This editorial correspondence is in Special Collections, University of Houston Library.

11. McMurtry, "Best Seller! A Novelist Looks at 'Verbal Evil' and the Presidential Transcripts as Bedside Reading," *Potomac, Washington Post*, 23, June 1974, pp. 12–13, 26–27.

12. Ibid., p. 27.

13. Ibid., p. 13.

14. Ibid., p. 26.

15. "Devilish Breakfast, Says Larry McMurtry," *Houston Post*, 23 Aug. 1968, sec. 3, p. 3.

16. McMurtry, "Your Place or Mine: Speculations on Female Macho," *Potomac, Washington Post*, 14, April 1974, pp. 12–13, 35–36.

17. Ibid., p. 35.

18. Ibid.

19. Ibid.

20. This is certainly not true, of course, of Vernon Dalhart, the shy, introverted, middle-aged virgin who is also an oil-rich millionaire. His speech is awkward, unsophisticated, and definitely "down home" in its dialect. When confronted by the urbane wit and sophisticated chatter of Aurora Greenway, he inevitably becomes inarticulate.

21. Interview with McMurtry, Oct. 1972, Washington, D.C.

22. McMurtry. "The Texas Moon, and Elsewhere," *Atlantic Monthly* (March 1975), p. 30.

23. "The Texas Moon," p. 34.

24. Ibid., p. 36.

25. Ibid., p. 34.

26. Ibid., p. 29.

27. Ibid., p. 31.

28. Ibid.

29. McMurtry later chronicled the changing face of Texas in a series of essays concerning tasteless architecture and the sprawling megopolis that Fort Worth and Dallas were becoming.

30. *Atlantic Monthly* (March 1975). McMurtry's essay, "The Texas Moon," appears on pages 29–36.

31. Ibid., p. 36.

Selected Bibliography

I McMurtry's Published Works

A. Fiction

All My Friends Are Going To Be Strangers. New York: Simon and Schuster, 1972.

"The Beginning of the Evening." *The Redneck Review,* (Spring 1968), 1–22. A note appended by McMurtry indicates this piece "is the first chapter of a long novel-in-progress called *The Country of the Horn*"; actually it is a variant version of the first chapter of *Moving On.*

"The Best Day Since." *Avesta,* 36 (Fall 1956), 32–36.

"Cowman." *Avesta* 37 (Spring 1957), 20–25.

"Dunlup Crashes In." *Playboy,* 22 (July 1975), 119, 144–154.

"A Fragment from Scarlet Ribbons." *Coexistence Review,* 1, No. 2 (n.d.).

"From the Prologue to *Horseman, Pass By." Coexistence Review,* 1, No. 1 (n.d.).

"Grandad's End: A Section from *Horseman, Pass By." Coexistence Review,* 1, No. 1 (n.d.).

Horseman, Pass By. New York: Harper & Brothers, 1961.

"Horseman, Pass By." *The Rice Mill,* 1 (Fall 1958), 5–8. Editor's note indicates "the following are two excerpts from a recently completed novel which Mr. McMurtry is now in the process of revising."

"Horseman, Pass By." *Southwest Review,* 46 (Spring 1961), 122–127. Variant version of text later published as the prologue to the novel of the same name.

Hud. New York: Popular Library, n.d. Paperback reissue of *Horseman, Pass By.*

The Last Picture Show. New York: Dial Press, 1966.

"The Last Picture Show." *Janus* (Fall 1965), 2–5. A selection from chapter 8 of the novel.

Leaving Cheyenne. New York: Harper & Row, 1963.

"Leaving Cheyenne." *Stanford Short Stories, 1962.* Stanford: Stanford Univ. Press, 1962, pp. 54–72. Contains excerpt from novel (then in

127

progress) but shows variations in text and in headnote from final pub-
lished version of *Leaving Cheyenne.*
Moving On. New York: Simon and Schuster, 1970.
"Roll, Jordan, Roll." *Avesta,* 38 (Fall 1957), 33–37.
Terms of Endearment. New York: Simon and Schuster, 1975.
"There Will Be Peace in Korea." *Texas Quarterly,* 7 (Winter 1964), 166–
170. Variant version of the incidents described in *The Last Picture
Show,* chapter 25.

B.   Poetry

"Credo." *Coexistence Review,* 1, No. 1 (n.d.).
"First Prize Winner." *Coexistence Review,* 1, No. 2 (n.d.).
"For Erwin Smith, Cowboy Photographer." *Southeast Review,* 45 (Winter
1960), 73.
"From 'The Watch-Fires.' " *Coexistence Review,* 1, No. 2 (n.d.).
"Quietus." *Avesta,* 37 (Fall 1957), 27.
"The Watch-Fires." *Coexistence Review,* 1, No. 1 (n.d.).
"Yes, I Am Old." *Avesta,* 37 (Spring 1957), 31.

C.   Nonfiction

"Answer from McMurtry." *Texas Observer,* 63 (26 Feb. 1971), 22–24. A
response to a hostile review of *Moving On.*
"The Beat Academy." *Janus* (Mar. 1960), 13–15, 28–31.
"Beiderbecke." *Avesta,* 37 (Spring 1957), 14–16.
"Cowboy." *Houston Post,* 26 May 1963, pp. 25, 28.
"Cowboys and Cadillacs: Realism in the Movies." *Riata* (Fall 1966), 4–9.
"Cowboys, Movies, Myths, and Cadillacs." *Janus* (Spring 1964), 3–7.
"Cowboys, Movies, Myths, and Cadillacs: Realism in the Western." In *Man
and the Movies,* ed. W. R. Robinson. Baton Rouge: Louisiana State
Univ. Press, 1967, pp. 46–52.
"Dallas: A Reflection." *Gentleman's Quarterly* (Mar. 1966), 128, 129, 154.
"Devilish Breakfast, says McMurtry." Letter to the editor of the *Houston
Post* attacking a *Post* editorial, "Hanoi's View of U.S. Fanciful." *Hous-
ton Post,* 23 Aug. 1968, Sec. 3, p. 3.
"Goat-Ropers and Groupies: A Requiem for a Rodeo," *New York,* 5 (27 Nov.
1972), 58–62.
In a Narrow Grave: Essays on Texas. Austin: Encino Press, 1968.
It's Always We Rambled: An Essay on Rodeo. New York: Frank Hallman,
1974.
"Journey to the End of the Road." *Avesta,* 37 (Fall 1957), 22–27.
"Love, Death, and the Astrodome." *The Texas Observer,* 1 Oct. 1965,
pp. 2–4.
"The Old Soldier's Joy: An Essay on the Annual Fiddler's Reunion Held in
Athens, Texas." *Texas Quarterly,* 6 (Autumn 1963), 166–176.

"Texas: Good Times Gone, or Here Again?" *Holiday*, 38 (Sept. 1965), 58–59, 75, 77–79.

"Best Seller! A Novelist Looks at 'Verbal Evil' and the Presidential Transcripts as Bedside Reading." *Potomac, Washington Post*, 23 June 1974, pp. 12–13, 26–27.

"The Texas Moon, and Elsewhere." *The Atlantic*, 235 (Mar. 1975), 29–36.

"Your Place or Mine: Speculations on Female Macho." *Potomac, Washington Post*, 14 April 1974, pp. 12–13, 35–36.

D. Film Criticism

"Approaching Cheyenne . . . Leaving Lumet. Oh, Pshaw!" *New York*, 7 (29 April 1974), 64–66.

"Cowboys and Cadillacs: Realism in the Movies." *Riata* (Fall 1966), 4–9.

"Cowboys, Movies, Myths, and Cadillacs." *Janus* (Spring 1964), 3–7.

"Cowboys, Movies, Myths, and Cadillacs: Realism in the Western." In *Man and the Movies*, ed. W. R. Robinson. Baton Rouge: Louisiana State Univ. Press, 1967, pp. 46–52.

"Cowboys, Movies, Myths, and Cadillacs: An Excursus on Ritual Forms in the Western Movie." In *In a Narrow Grave*. Austin: Encino Press, 1968, pp. 21–29.

"The Deadline Syndrome." *American Film*, 1 (Dec. 1975), 4–5, 69.

"Finding the Film." *American Film*, 1 (May 1976), 6–7, 74.

"The Fun of It All." *American Film*, 1 (April 1976), 54–55, 90.

"The Hired Pen." *American Film*, 1 (Nov. 1975), 4–5, 71.

"The Last Picture Show: A Last Word." *Colonial Times*, 1 (21 Dec. – 12 Jan. 1972), 1, 14.

"The Last Word on 'The Last Picture Show.' " *The Daily Rag*, 1, No. 1 (Oct. 1972), 13.

"Movie Tripping: My Own Rotten Film Festival." *New York*, (6 Feb. 1973), 38–49.

"No Clue, or Learning to Write for the Movies." *American Film*, 1 (Oct. 1975), 9–12.

"Personal Factors." *American Film*, 1 (Mar. 1976), 6–7, 73.

"Properties, Projects, Possibilities." *American Film*, 1 (June 1976), 6–7, 79.

"The Telephone Booth Screenwriter." *American Film*, 1 (Jan.–Feb. 1976), 8–9, 65.

E. Book Reviews

Because McMurtry's reviews are so numerous, they are listed alphabetically by author, with the dates on which they appeared.

Houston Post

James Agee, *Letters to Father Flye*, 29 July 1962; Nelson Algren, *Who Lost an American*, 19 May 1963; Alfred Andersch, *The Night of the Giraffe*,

13 Dec. 1964; Machado de Assis, *Esau and Jacob*, 15 Aug. 1965; Louis Auchincloss, *Tales of Manhattan*, 19 Mar. 1967; Richard Bankowski, *On a Dark Night*, 14 June 1964;John Barth, *Giles Goat Boy*, 7 Aug. 1966; Samuel Beckett, *How It Is*, 8 Mar. 1964; Saul Bellow, *Herzog*, 20 Sept. 1964; Jack Bennett, *Mister Fisherman*, 14 Feb. 1965; Thomas Berger, *Little Big Man*, 18 Oct. 1964; Wendell Berry, *November Twenty-Six Nineteen Hundred Sixty-Three*, 24 May 1964; Harold Bienvenu, *The Patriot*, 29 Nov. 1964; Burt Blechman, *Stations*, 29 Nov. 1964; Richard Brautigan, *A Confederate General from Big Sur*, 24 Jan. 1965; Harvey Breit, *A Narrow Action*, 14 June 1964; Mikhail Bulgakov, *Black Snow*, 21 April 1968; Anthony Burgess, *The Long Day Wanes*, 2 May 1965; Anthony Burgess, *Rejoyce*, 5 Dec. 1965; William Burroughs, *Naked Lunch*, 25 Nov. 1962; William Burroughs, *Nova Express*, Nov. 1964; William Burroughs, *The Soft Machine*, 12 Mar. 1966; William Burroughs, *The Ticket That Exploded*, 11 June 1967; O.A. Bushnell, *Molokai*, 10 Nov. 1963; George Byrams, *Tomorrow's Hidden Season*, 6 Sept. 1964; Elias Canetti, *Auto-Da-Fe*, 8 Mar. 1964; John Stewart Carter, *Full Fathom Five*, 14 Feb. 1965; Henry Cecil, *Portrait of a Judge*, 14 Feb. 1965; Louis Ferdinand Celine, *Death on the Installment Plan*, 25 Dec. 1966; Fred Chappell, *The Inkling*, Aug 1965; Driss ben Hamed Charhadi, *A Life Full of Holes*, 3 May 1964; Alfred Chester, *The Exquisite Corpse*, 19 Mar. 1967; Larry Collins and Dominique Lapierre, *Is Paris Burning?* 20 June 1965; John William Corrington, *And Wait for the Night*, 31 May 1964; John William Corrington, *Anatomy of Love and Other Poems*, 21 June 1964; J. P. Donleavy, *The Saddest Summer of Samuel S.*, 12 Mar. 1966; H.E.F. Donohue, *The Higher Animals*, 14 Feb. 1965; Marguerite Duras, *Four Novels*, 28 Nov. 1965; Friedrich Durrenmatt, *Once a Greek*, 30 May 1965; Ilya Ehrenburg, *The War, 1941–1945*, 18 July 1965; George P. Elliott, *A Piece of Lettuce*, 22 Mar. 1964; Seymour Epstein, *Leah*, 5 July 1964; Peter Everett, *Negatives*, 16 May 1965; Constantine Fitzgibbon, *The Life of Dylan Thomas*, 7 Nov. 1965; Jean Genet, *Miracle of the Rose*, 19 Feb. 1967; John Bart Gerald, *A Thousand Mornings*, 12 Jan. 1964; José Maria Gironella, *One Million Dead*, 22 Dec. 1963; Herbert Gold, *Salt*, 14 April 1963; Herbert Gold, *Fathers*, 19 Mar. 1967; William Golding, *The Inheritors*, 5 Aug. 1962; William Goldman, *Boys and Girls Together*, 5 July 1964; Witold Gombrowica, *Ferdydurke and Pornographia*, 21 May 1967; Bill Gunn, *All the Rest Have Died*, 15 Nov. 1964; A. B. Guthrie, Jr. *The Blue Hen's Chick*, 23 May 1965; Ben Haas, *Look Away, Look Away*, 19 July 1964; James Baker Hall, *Yates Paul, His Grand Flights, His Tootings*, 22 Sept. 1963; James B. Hall, *Us He Devours*, 29 Nov. 1964; William Harrison, *The Theologian*, 26 Sept. 1965; John Hawkes, *Second Skin*, 5 April 1964; Hiram Hayden, *The Hounds of Esau*, 27 May 1962; Joseph

Hayes, *The Third Day*, 6 Sept. 1964; Erich Heller, *The Artist's Journey into the Interior*, 5 Dec. 1965; James Leo Herlihy, *Midnight Cowboy*, 29 Aug. 1965; Herman Hesse, *Demian*, 13 June 1965; Robert E. Howard, *A Gent from Bear Creek*, 20 Mar. 1966; Rodello Hunter, *A House of Many Rooms*, 22 Aug. 1965; John Iggluden, *The Clouded Sky*, 6 Sept. 1964; Randall Jarrell, *The Lost World*, 14 Mar. 1965; James Jones, *Go to the Widowmaker*, 23 April 1967; Leroi Jones, *The System of Dante's Hell*, 28 Nov. 1965; Cheikh Hamidon Kane, *Ambiguous Adventure*, 12 Jan. 1964; Ken Kesey, *One Flew over the Cuckoo's Nest*, 18 Mar. 1962; Ken Kesey, *Sometimes a Great Notion*, 12 July 1964; Marcus Klein, *After Alienation*, 27 Sept. 1964; Richard Kluger, *When the Bough Breaks*, 19 July 1964; W. S. Kuniczak, *The Thousand Hour Day*, 11 June 1967; Phillip Larkin, *The Whitsun Weddings*, 8 Nov. 1964; Jeremy Larner, *Drive, He Said*, 15 Nov. 1964; John Lennon, *A Spaniard in the Works*, 11 July 1965; Robert W. Lewis, *Hemingway on Love*, 5 Dec. 1965; Edward Loomis, *Men of Principle*, 24 Feb. 1963; Robert Lowell, *For the Union Dead*, 8 Nov. 1964; Mochtar Lubis, *Twilight in Djakarta*, 3 May 1964; Josef Machiewicz, *Road to Nowhere*, 2 Aug. 1964; Norman Mailer, *An American Dream*, 7 Mar. 1965; Bernard Malamud, *Idiots First*, 24 Nov. 1963; Richard McKenna, *The Sand Pebbles*, 16 Dec. 1962; H. D. Miller, *The Great Sweet Days of Old Shibui*, 19 July 1964; Henry Miller, *Tropic of Capricorn*, 9 Sept. 1962; Henry Miller, *Sexus*, 4 June 1965; Warren Miller, *Looking for the General*, 12 Jan. 1964; Alberto Moravia, *The Fetish*, 2 May 1965; Arthur Mizener, *The Sense of Life in the Modern Novel*, 5 April 1964; Wlodzimierz Odojewski, *The Dying Day*, 3 May 1964; Charles Perry, *Portrait of a Young Man Drowning*, 22 April 1962; Ben Piaza, *The Exact and Very Strange Truth*, 2 Aug. 1964; Norman Podhoretz, *Doings and Undoings*, 22 Mar. 1964; Norman Podhoretz, *Making It*, 21 Jan. 1968; Pandelis Prevelakis, *The Sun of Death*, 13 Dec. 1964; Frederic Prokosch, *The Dark Dancer*, 15 April 1964; Raja Rao, *The Serpent and the Rope*, 27 Jan. 1963; John Rechy, *City of Night*, 9 June 1963; Frank Reynolds, *Freewheelin' Frank: Secretary of the Angels*, 22 Oct. 1967; Conrad Richter, *The Grandfathers*, 14 June 1964; Don Robertson, *Westwind*, 2 Aug. 1964; Philip Roth, *Letting Go*, 3 June 1962; Leonard Sanders, *The Wooden Horseshoe*, 7 June 1964; Stephen Schneck, *The Nightclerk*, 10 Oct. 1965; Paul Scott, *The Corrida at San Feliu*, 10 Jan. 1965; Vincent Sheean, *Beware of Caesar*, 11 July 1965; Wilfred Sheed, *Square's Progress*, 22 Aug. 1965; Alan Sillitoe, *Key to the Door*, 13 May 1962; Alexander Solzhenitsyn, *For the Good of the Cause*, 5 July 1964; Susan Sontag, *Against Interpretation*, 30 Jan. 1966; Wallace Stegner, *Wolf Willow*, 28 Oct. 1962; Richard Martin Stern, *Right Hand Opposite*, 12 Jan. 1964; Harvey Swados, *The Will*, 24 Nov. 1963; Philip Toynbee, *Two Brothers*, 14 Mar. 1965; John Updike,

Couples, 14 April 1968; Stephen Vizinzey, *In Praise of Older Women*, 12 Mar. 1966; John Wain, *Strike the Father Dead*, 14 Oct. 1962; Robert Penn Warren, *Who Speaks for the Negro*, 4 June 1965; Constance Webb, *Richard Wright*, 31 Mar. 1968; James Webb and A. Wigfall Green, *William Faulkner of Oxford*, 3 Oct. 1965; Thornton Wilder, *The Eighth Day*, 16 April 1967; Jonathan Williams, *Lines About Hills above Lakes*, 21 June 1964; Vinnie Williams, *I Resign You, Stallion*, 14 Feb. 1965; Calder Willingham, *Eternal Fire*, 20 Jan. 1963; Sloan Wilson, *Georgie Winthrop*, 13 Jan. 1963; Bernard Wolfe, *Come On Out Daddy*, 13 Oct. 1963; Richard Yates, *Eleven Kinds of Loneliness*, 13 May 1962.

New York Times

Warren Farrell, *The Liberated Man*, 5 Jan. 1975; Marc Feigen Fasteau, *The Male Machine*, 5 Jan. 1975; George Gilder, *Naked Nomads*, 5 Jan. 1975.

Saturday Review

Vardis Fisher, *Mountain Man*, 6 Nov. 1955.

Washington Post

Patrick Anderson, *The Approach to Kings*, 14 Oct. 1970; Ingmar Bergman, *Scenes from a Marriage*, translated from the Swedish by A. Blair, 26 Aug. 1974; Wendell Berry, *The Hidden Wound*, 19 Oct. 1970; Wendell Berry, *Farming: A Hand Book*, 19 Oct. 1970; James Blake, *The Joint*, 21 Mar. 1971; John Braine, *Writing a Novel*, 11 Nov. 1974; Richard Brautigan, *The Hawkline Monster: A Gothic Western*, 9 Sept. 1974; James Lee Burke, *Lay Down My Sword and Shield*, 5 Feb. 1972; Tony Buttitta, *After the Good Gay Times: Ashville—Summer of '35. A Season with F. Scott Fitzgerald*, 17 June 1974; José Luis Castillo-Puche, *Hemingway in Spain: A Personal Reminiscence of Hemingway's Years in Spain by His Friend*, 17 June 1974; Colette, *Retreat from Love*, translated from the French with an introduction by Margaret Grosland, 5 Aug. 1974; J. P. Donleavy, *The Onion Eaters*, 26 July 1971; T. R. Fehrenbach, *Comanches: The Destruction of a People*, 9 Dec. 1974; Frederick Forsyth, *The Day of the Jackal*, 19 Aug. 1971; Maria Friedman, *The Story of Josh*, 30 Dec. 1974; Norman Fruman, *Coleridge, The Damaged Archangel*, 18 Jan. 1972; Timothy Gallwey, *The Inner Game of Tennis*, 3 June 1974; George Garrett, *Death of the Fox*, 20 Oct. 1971; Gail Godwin, *The Odd Woman*, 21 Oct. 1974; Shirley Ann Grau, *The Condor Passes*, 22 Sept. 1971; Bernard Grebanier, *The Uninhibited Byron: An Account of His Sexual Confusion*, 23 Nov. 1970; Hiram Haydn, *Words and Faces*, 28 Oct. 1974; Philip Henderson, *Portrait of a Poet*, 16 Sept. 1974; Rust Hills, ed., *Writers Choice*,

16 Dec. 1974; Daniel Hoffman, *Poe Poe Poe Poe Poe Poe Poe*, 19 Feb. 1972; Cecilia Hollands, *Great Maria*, 23 Dec. 1974; James Jones, *The Merry Month of May*, 15 Feb. 1971; Ron Kurz, *Lethal Gas*, 25 Nov. 1974; John Lahr, *Hot to Trot*, 4 Nov. 1974; John LaCarré, *The Naive and Sentimental Lover*, 3 Jan. 1972; Ella Leftland, *Love Out of Season*, 23 Sept. 1974; Grace Lichtenstein, *A Long Way Baby: Behind the Scenes in Women's Pro Tennis*, 3 June 1974; Dorothy Michelson Livingston, *The Master of Light: A Biography of Albert A. Michelson*, 24 June 1974; Anita Loos, *Kiss Hollywood Good-By*, 22 July 1974; Doris Lund, *Eric*, 30 Dec. 1974; Charles A. Madison, *Irving to Irving: Author-Publisher Relations: 1800–1974*, 28 Oct. 1974; Leslie A. Marchand, *Byron: A Portrait*, 23 Nov. 1970; Mary McCarthy, *Birds of America*, 1 June 1971; Dwight Macdonald, *Discriminations*, 7 Oct. 1974; John McClusky, *Look What They Done to My Song*, 4 Nov. 1974; Patricia Taylert McIvers, *Good Night, Mr. Christopher*, 30 Dec. 1974; Michael Mewshaw, *Man in Motion*, 3 Oct. 1970; Michael Meyer, *Ibsen: A Biography*, 28 Sept. 1971; Kate Millett, *Flying*, 10 June 1974; Penelope Mortimer, *The Home*, 7 Mar. 1972; Malcolm Muggeridge, *Chronicles of Wasted Time: Chronicle 2: The Infernal Grove*, 29 July 1974; John O'Hara, *The Good Samaritan and Other Stories*, 19 Aug. 1974; V. S. Pritchett, *The Camberwell Beauty and Other Stories*, 30 Sept. 1974; Maria Rofheart, *My Name is Sappho*, 23 Dec. 1974; Gilbert Rogin, *What Happens Next Time?* 5 Feb. 1972; Joseph Roth, *The Radetzky March*, translated by Eva Tucker, 2 Sept. 1974; Irwin Shaw, *Rich Man, Poor Man*, 25 Sept. 1970; James R. Smith and Lynn G. Smith, *Beyond Monogamy: Recent Studies of Sexual Alternatives in Marriage*, 12 Aug. 1974; Mary Lee Spence and Donald Jackson, eds., *The Expeditions of Charles Frémont*, 8 July 1974; Michael Stevens, *V. Sackville-West, A Critical Biography*, 15 July 1974; Edith Summers, *The Devil's Hand*, 14 Oct. 1974; Gillian Tindall, *The Born Exile*, 2 Dec. 1974; Leon Uris, *QB VII*, 6 April 1971; Raoul Walsh, *Each Man In His Time: The Life Story of a Director*, 26 Aug. 1974; Peter Whittaker, *The American Way of Sex*, 12 Aug. 1974; William Wright, *The Washington Game*, 18 Nov. 1974.

II McMurtry Manuscripts and
Letters in the Special Collection Room at the University
of Houston Library

A.   Editorial Correspondence

The collection of McMurtry material at the University of Houston includes an extensive file of editorial correspondence concerning *Horseman, Pass By* and *Leaving Cheyenne*. These letters are particularly significant; they show what changes McMurtry would (and would not) make in his manuscripts before they were published by Harpers. Some of the more interesting correspondence is:

John Howard Griffin to Jack Leggett of Harper and Brothers, 20 Mar. 1961, 1 page. Praises McMurtry's first novel.

A. B. Guthrie, Jr., with manuscript P.S., to John Leggett of Harper and Brothers, 15 May 1961, 1 page. Praises McMurtry.

John Leggett to Larry McMurtry, 7 April 1960, 3 pages. Suggests extensive revisions of *Horseman*. Refers to many incidents not in published version, for example, a cyclone, a confrontation between Hud and Homer in a storm cellar, an argument over a checker game.

Leggett to McMurtry, 10 May 1960, 1 page. Suggests that McMurtry concentrate on Lonnie as the focal character: "There's something awfully appealing about an adolescent for a viewpoint character." Also states that McMurtry is wise in deciding to use the third-person narrative because it "allows maximum freedom and yet permits as much subjectiveness as you want to give it."

Leggett to McMurtry, 16 June 1960, 2 pages. Suggests changes, many of which were incorporated in published version.

Leggett to McMurtry, 23 Aug. 1960, 5 pages. Important letter; suggests many changes in the character of Lonnie and lists suggested deletions from Lonnie's dialogue (many of a sexual or obscene nature). The deletions are designed to preserve Lonnie's essential innocence for the reader. McMurtry apparently acquiesced.

Other Leggett letters of interest involve suggested revisions in the rape scene in *Horseman, Pass By*; see particularly 27 Oct., 15 Nov., 30 Nov. 1960.

Leggett to McMurtry, 24 Feb. 1961, 1 page. Initial impressions of *Our Revels Now Are Ended* (original title of *Leaving Cheyenne*).

Leggett to McMurtry, 6 July 1964. 2 pages. Negative reaction to McMurtry's novel, *Lovebreaking*.

B   Kunkel Collection

The Kunkel Collection of McMurtry letters and manuscripts is contained in one box in the Special Collections room at the University of Houston. All items listed below (unless otherwise noted) are letters from McMurtry to Kunkel. The Kunkel Collection was acquired from Mike Kunkel, a friend of McMurtry, in August 1967.

Two stories, in envelope bearing uncancelled stamp, addressed to Mike Kunkel, 1210 Lamb, Bowie, Texas. Return address is Larry McMurtry, 1120 West Congress, Denton, Texas. Three-line note accompanies stories: "The Untrodden Ways," seven-page carbon typescript, and "Lonely Singer, Lonely Song," six-page carbon typescript, another version of the story about the retarded boy who sits on the floor of a bookstore. Cf. fragment: "Scarlet Ribbons."

Postmarked Denton, 15 July 1957. Return address, Larry McMurtry, Box 552, Archer City, Texas. Two-page typed letter to Kunkel in which McMurtry discusses his recent writing. Mentions that he would like to do a one-act dramatization of Faulkner's "That Evening Sun Go Down" [*sic*] and that he has been much influenced by Faulkner. Two-page poem, "Firebird . . . An Elegy," accompanies letter.

Postmarked Denton, 11 Nov. 1956, 2 pages. Discusses McMurtry's book collecting and his studies at Rice. McMurtry states that he has "despaired of ever writing publishable short stories, and have thrice started a novel," which "never gets beyond 20 pages." Enclosed with letter is McMurtry's own answers to Margaret Anderson's questionnaire, which was mailed to the famous contributors of her *Little Review* (3 pages).

Postmarked Houston, 24 Jan. 1956, 2 pages. Comments on McMurtry's latest writing: "Several essays, some light, some pompous, and one biographical," and "some lyric poetry." Letter also contains comments on Archer City: "Archer City is rather a mess. If I didn't love the place I'd hate it violently. A bunch of almost inextricably mixed up kids." One-page poem, "Lonely sachem, gone . . . ." is enclosed with letter.

Five short stories: "The Promise and the Pledge." Nine-page carbon typescript. In manuscript accompanying story, McMurtry says, "The first thing of any consequence I wrote. The writing, especially in the stream of consciousness is about as good as I've done." "Angels Near the Star: A Prelude to Remembrance." Seven-page carbon typescript. Manuscript note to Kunkel accompanies story. "Cowboys Wear Spurs." Eight-page carbon typescript, accompanied by manuscript note to Kunkel. "This Moment Removed." Three-page carbon typescript, accompanied by manuscript note to Kunkel. "A Gleam in the dust." Five-page carbon typescript accompanied by manuscript note to Kunkel.

Postmarked Houston, 3 Dec. 1955, 2 pages. Mentions his disillusionment with Rice University: "a vastly overrated aggregation of uppermiddle class snobs and first rate psychopaths"; his "agnosticism"; his desire to write a novel.

Postmarked Houston, 9 Dec. 1955, 2 pages. Mentions his recent reading and his impression of John Steinbeck.

Postmarked Denton, 12 Mar. 1956, 1 page.

Postmarked Denton, 21 Mar. 1956, 1 page. About book-buying expedition mentioned in letter of 12 Mar.

Postmarked Archer City, 31 Aug. 1956, 2 pages, 4 manuscript pages. Lists books (with brief comments) recently read. Comments on his renewed interest in philosophy. Says he has lost interest in "obscurantist school"

("Pound, Joyce, Eliot"). Says Joyce "forfeited a great deal of art to vocabulary, and Eliot a great deal of music to erudition." One of the more important letters in the collection. Contains his views on religion.

Postmarked Denton, 18 Nov. 1956, 2 pages. Mentions experience in a Dallas bookstore, where a retarded boy sat on the floor and sang and was mistreated by his mother. Incident used later in two stories.

Postmarked Denton, 20 Jan. 1957, 3 pages. Concerned with book-buying adventures and revised views of Faulkner and T. S. Eliot.

Postmarked Denton, 19 Mar. 1957, 5-line note. Indicates his increasing disaffection for Archer City. Contains many comments on literature.

Postmarked Archer City, 27 Aug. 1957, 2 pages. Indicates his desire to write poetry rather than fiction.

Postmarked Archer City, Aug. 1955, 3 pages, manuscript. Last page apparently missing. Return address on envelope given as "Paradise Enow" [(Archer City later called "Thalia" in *The Last Picture Show*.)]

Postmarked 14 Aug. 1955, 3 pages, manuscript. Contains much that would indicate how autobiographical certain aspects of *Leaving Cheyenne* and *The Last Picture Show* are.

Postmarked Houston, 19 Sept. 1955, 2 pages, manuscript. 1955. Lists courses he is taking at Rice University.

Postmarked Houston, 30 Sept. 1955, 8 pages, manuscript. Describes his job at the public library, his courses at Rice, his recent reading.

Postmarked 4 Nov. 1955, 2 pages, manuscript. Mentions that his creative-writing teacher advises him to write of his "world" (i.e., Archer City). "So, so will I. I don't think (or expect) it'll sell though—."

Postmarked Houston, 20 Oct. 1955, 4 pages, manuscript. Written in a very depressed state. Indicates his increasing disenchantment with Rice. Mentions that short story "Angels Near the Star" is "most autobiographical."

Postmarked Archer City, 5 July 1956, 2 pages, manuscript. Mentions that he is at work on a sonnet sequence and two short stories, "Lonely Stars, Pretty Stars" and "The Father of God." Mentions his "current idol" is Nietzsche. Contains much comment on his recent reading. Expresses his discontent with North Texas State.

C. Unpublished Material

"Breeding Darrell." Typescript of unpublished story, 6½ pages. A greatly revised version was incorporated into *The Last Picture Show* (chapter 10). Copy in Special Collections Room, University of Houston Library.

"Evening Song." Typescript of unpublished poem, 1 page. Signed "Valentine Day, '58" in McMurtry's hand.

"For John Lewis, divine." Typescript of unpublished poem, 1 page. Note in McMurtry's hand indicates poem was completed in 1958.

"Jesse and the Buyer." Typescript of unpublished short story, 8 pages. Notation in McMurtry's hand reads "circa 1954/LM 1965."

"Leaving Cheyenne: Essays on American Rodeo." Ditto outline, 3 pages of a book to be "fifty to sixty thousand words; twelve to fourteen chapters of four to five thousand words each." McMurtry's note says, "I drew up the enclosed outline in 1962 and traveled some 7,000 miles before giving up on the book." Contained in folder with three pages of manuscript notes by McMurtry regarding book's format, illustrations, riders he wanted to interview.

Lovebreaking. Typescript of novel, with manuscript corrections, 574 pages. McMurtry's note indicates that this is the third draft of the novel completed in spring 1965. Note reads "Abandoned Spring, 1965; now in revison as *The Country of the Horn.*"

Our Revels Now Are Ended. Typescript of uncompleted novel, 2 chapters: chapter 1, pp. 1–18; chapter 2, pp. 19–41. Manuscript note in McMurtry's hand indicates that this represents "2 chapters of an abandoned novel" and that it dates from "late 1961–early 1962. It was written while McMurtry was at Stanford University.

"A Primer of Post-War Fiction (Outline)." Typescript, 3 pages. Included in same folder is another typescript (2 pages), which is either another outline or a tentative table of contents. Also in the same folder is a typescript (5 pages) of an introduction and 64 pages of text. McMurtry's note on folder indicates that "A Primer of Post-War Fiction" was written and abandoned in 1963–1964.

"A Primer of Post-War Fiction (Outline)." Typescript, 2 pages. Another outline or tentative table of contents.

Prospectus for Thalia Stories. One page of manuscript in college "blue book".

"The Questions a Writer Gets Asked." Typescript, 12 pages, and manuscript, 1 page, of an unpublished speech. McMurtry's pencil notation on page 1 says, "This speech has been delivered 17 times to date—1968."

"The Questions a Writer Gets Asked." Typescript, 20 pages. Variant text of above entry.

"Reliving My Days in High School." Freshman English 101 theme, 2 pages.

"Scraps." Typescript, 43 pages. Outline and various insertions to be included in *Leaving Cheyenne.* Not all of this material was used in the novel.

Spawn of Evil. Typescript of screenplay, 357 pages. First draft dates from May–June 1965.

"Spawn of Evil—A Synopsis." Typescript, 134 pages. McMurtry's note indicates this is a brief treatment of the new story to be included in the original screenplay (see above). Dated July 1965.

The Thalia Stores—III. "The Everlasting Arms." Typescript with manuscript corrections, 12 pages. Note indicates it was written at Stanford.

The Thalia Stores—III. "Breeding Darrell." Typescript with manuscript corrections, 8 pages.

Thesis, Master's, Rice University, Houston, Texas. 1958–1959. "Ben Jonson's Feud with the Poetasters, 1599–1601." 88 pages plus 5 pages of bibliography.

Untitled novel. Typescript, 299 pages with manuscript corrections. A revision (second draft) of the *Water and the Blood*. McMurtry's note indicates that this is second draft of the novel. Completed Dec. 1964.

"The Watch-Fires—for the Old Men on the Square." Typescript of unpublished poem, 1 page. Note in McMurtry's hand indicates poem was completed in 1958.

"The Watch-Fires." Carbon copy of typescript of unpublished version of poem. Title page, with two-line quotation from Hart Crane, plus eight unnumbered pages of verse. In the possession of Grover Lewis, Houston, Texas. Copy in the University of Houston Library.

The Water and the Blood. A Melodramatic Novel. Typescript of novel, with manuscript corrections, 301 pages. (Working title later changed to *Country of the Horns*.) Note in pencil indicates that this was written in the summer and fall of 1964.

"The Writer in Texas." Folder containing two college "blue books" (examination booklets). Booklets contain random notes. Folder also contains 2 pages of typed notes on J. Frank Dobie.

D.   Published Material

The Cowboy's Lament: An Essay on Texas. Typescript, 271 pages. Manuscript note indicates this is a second draft, finished in Archer City, Texas, on Christmas 1967. The book was to be published as *In a Narrow Grave* in September 1968.

"Cowboys, Movies, Myths, and Cadillacs: Realism in the Western." Typescript with manuscript corrections, 13 pages.

"Dallas: A Reflection." Typescript of the *Gentleman's Quarterly* article, 10 pages, 7 March 1966.

"Houston—Alphabetically Considered." Typescript, 35 pages. McMurtry notes that this is the first draft and dates from late 1965. Contained in folder with various chamber of commerce folders about Houston and two letters from Stephan Wilkinson (senior editor of *Holiday* magazine) about possibility of publishing manuscript in *Holiday*.

"Houston: City in the Making." Typescript, 33 pages. Second draft of Houston article (see above with manuscript corrections).

"Houston: City in the Making." Copy, 35 pages, of third draft of Houston article, with manuscript corrections in ink, constituting a fourth and final draft. Included in *In a Narrow Grave*.

"LSD: Why? What It Means to Some People Who Take It and Some Who Don't." Typescript of interview on LSD with Miriam Kass of the *Hous-*

ton Post, 5 pages. Attached to typed note (1 page) to Miriam Kass regarding above. Signed in red ink. Also 3 pages (typed) of questions from Miriam Kass for above interview.

The Last Picture Show. Typescript of novel, 500 pages. Manuscript note indicates that this was agent's copy of the novel and that it was completed Dec. 1965.

[*The Last Picture-Show*.] Typescript of the novel *The Last Picture Show*, 468 pages. Lacks title page. Has manuscript corrections.

Leaving Cheyenne. Typescript. 2 drafts, irregularly paginated: one draft 180 pages; another (missing book I), 97 pages.

Memories of the Old Tribe. Typescript with manuscript corrections, 197 pages. First draft of novel that was later retitled *Leaving Cheyenne*.

"The Old Soldier's Joy—An Essay on the Old Fiddler's Reunion held annually in Athens, Texas." Carbon typescript with manuscript corrections, 26 pages. Published in *Texas Quarterly*. 6 (Autumn 1963), 166–176.

"Texas From Stem to Stern." Five drafts—all typescripts with corrections. Draft 1 has variant title: "Texas from Stern to Stem." 33 pages with manuscript corrections. Draft 2: same title, 33 pages with manuscript corrections. Draft 3: same title, 31 pages with manuscript corrections; letter from Wilkinson, suggesting revision, attached (2 pages). Draft 4 "Texas From Stem to Stern": 20 typed pages (1 page in manuscript) with manuscript corrections; attached is a letter (2 pages) from Stephan Wilkinson, senior editor of *Holiday*, suggesting revisions. Draft 4: another copy; Draft 5: the accepted version (22 pages); published as *Holiday* article, "Texas: Good Times Gone, or Here Again?"

SECONDARY SOURCES

A. Articles

DAVIS, KENNETH W. "The Themes of Initiation in the Works of Larry McMurtry and Tom Mayer." *The Arlington Quarterly*, 2 (Winter 1969–1970), 29–43. Article stresses the importance of "place" or region in the initiatory forces (sex, stamina, and death) that propel the protagonists of McMurtry and Mayer toward maturation.

DEGENFELDER, E. PAULINE. "McMurtry and the Movies: *Hud* and *The Last Picture Show*." *Western Humanities Review*, 29 (Winter 1975), 81–91. A discussion of the movie adaptations of McMurtry's *Horseman, Pass By* and *The Last Picture Show*. Degenfelder argues that the stylistic difference between *Horseman, Pass By* and *The Last Picture Show* indicates that McMurtry was "consciously moving toward a more cinematic prose."

FOLSOM, JAMES K. "Shane and Hud: Two Stories in Search of a Medium." *Western Humanities Review*, 29 (Autumn 1970), 359–372. A discussion of the difficulties in transferring the mood of *Horseman, Pass By* to *Hud* and the "total reversal of the ending" of the novel in the cinema adaptation.

GILES, JAMES R. "Larry McMurtry's Leaving Cheyenne and the Novels of John Rechy: Four Trips Along 'the Mythical Pecos.' " *Forum* (Summer–Fall 1972), 35–40. Giles argues that McMurtry's *In a Narrow Grave* not only represents "a literary Declaration of Independence for the Texas writer from those restrictions of language and subject matter that so confined Dobie, Webb, and Bedichek" but is also "a complex theory about the relationship of the end of Texas' physical frontier and future explorations into its literary frontiers."

LANDESS, THOMAS. *Larry McMurtry*. Steck-Vaughn Company, Austin, 1969. An early assessment of McMurtry's work, with particular emphasis on his collection of essays, *In a Narrow Grave*.

PEAVY, CHARLES D. "A Larry McMurtry Bibliography." *Western American Literature*, 3 (Fall 1968), 235–248. A definitive bibliography of McMurtry's work published before 1968; includes fiction, essays, book reviews, unpublished works, and correspondence.

———. "Coming of Age in the Southwest: The Novels of Larry McMurtry." *Western American Literature*, 4 (Fall 1969), 171–188. An examination of the loss of innocence through sexual experience in the lives of McMurtry's male protagonists in *Horseman, Pass By, Leaving Cheyenne*, and *The Last Picture Show*.

———. "Larry McMurtry and Black Humor: A Note on *The Last Picture Show*." *Western American Literature*, 2 (Fall 1967), 223–227. An examination of McMurtry's use of black humor in his satiric examination of small-town morality.

PILKINGTON, WILLIAM T. "The Dirt Farmer and the Cowboy: Notes on Two Texas Essayists." *Re: Arts and Letters*, 3 (Fall 1969), 42–54. Reprinted in *My Blood's Country: Studies in Southwestern Literature*. Fort Worth, 1973, 163–182. Article contrasts McMurtry's *In a Narrow Grave* with Larry King's *And Other Dirty Stories* and examines the two writers' views of their native state from the differing perspectives of their background.

———. "The Recent Southwestern Novel." *Southwestern American Literature*, 1 (Jan. 1971), 12–15. Pilkington sees McMurtry as the major talent among the young Southwestern writers and the novelist who best describes the major social problem of the region: the "imperfect transition from a rural to an urban society."

SONNICHSEN, C. L. "The New-Style Western." *South Dakota Review*, 4 (Summer 1966), 22–28. Mentions McMurtry briefly in the context of contemporary Western fiction.

STOUT, JANIS P. "Journeying as a Metaphor: Cultural Loss in the Novels of Larry McMurtry." *Western American Literature*, 11 (May 1976),

37–50. Stout examines the gradual dominance of the automobile in McMurtry's novels and the cultural dissolution this dominance signifies.

B. Theses

ALLEN, ELIZABETH. "Leaving Cheyenne: The Evolution of the Cowboy in Larry McMurtry's Fiction." Master's thesis, Southwest Texas State University, 1975. Allen traces the evolution of the cowboy in specific McMurtry characters in the roles of the cattleman, the cowhand, the rodeo cowboy, and the symbolic cowboy and shows how each of these types has been "corrupted and changed" by sociological and technological pressures of the twentieth century.

SNIFFEN, JIMMIE CLIFTON. "The Emergence of Woman in the Novels of Larry McMurtry." Master's thesis, Stephen F. Austin State University, 1972. Sniffen contends that a study of the mythological, sociological, and psychological aspects of McMurtry's novels reveals that the female characters emerge as increasingly important to the novels and to the changing west Texas society the works depict.

TOVAR, INEZ HERNANDEZ. "The Quest Theme in the Fiction of Larry McMurtry." Master's thesis, University of Houston, 1972. Tovar argues that the quest for maturity and manhood of McMurtry's male characters is distinguished by the importance he places on the role the female figure plays in this quest.

Index